# Windows 95 explained

# ALSO AVAILABLE

# Windows 95 explained

by

**P.R.M. Oliver**
**and**
**N. Kantaris**

**BERNARD BABANI (publishing) LTD.**
**THE GRAMPIANS**
**SHEPHERDS BUSH ROAD**
**LONDON W6 7NF**
**ENGLAND**

# PLEASE NOTE

Although every care has been taken with the production of this book to ensure that any projects, designs, modifications and/or programs, etc., contained herewith, operate in a correct and safe manner and also that any components specified are normally available in Great Britain, the Publishers and Author(s) do not accept responsibility in any way for the failure (including fault in design) of any project, design, modification or program to work correctly or to cause damage to any equipment that it may be connected to or used in conjunction with, or in respect of any other damage or injury that may be so caused, nor do the Publishers accept responsibility in any way for the failure to obtain specified components.

Notice is also given that if equipment that is still under warranty is modified in any way or used or connected with home-built equipment then that warranty may be void.

First Published - November 1995

British Library Cataloguing in Publication Data:

Oliver, Phil
    Windows 95 Explained

    I. Title II. Kantaris, Noel
    005.43

    ISBN 0 85934 400 2

Printed and Bound in Great Britain by Cox & Wyman Ltd, Reading

# PREFACE

Microsoft produced the first version of Windows in 1983 as a graphical extension to MS-DOS. It was not a great success, being DOS based it was confined to the DOS memory limit of 1MB of RAM. Mind you, at that time, not many PCs even had that much memory.

A 386 specific version was brought out in 1987 that was able to run in multiple 'virtual 8086' mode, but Windows applications were still unable to use any extended memory above the 1MB.

In 1990 Windows 3.0 solved this problem and became a huge success for Microsoft, and of course, for Bill Gates. The much needed update, version 3.1, was released in April 1992 to fix most of the program bugs. The horrendous Unrecoverable Application Error message became a thing of the past with this release.

Windows for Workgroups 3.1, in October 1992, started to give the program the power to control small networked groups of computers. This was strengthened in October 1993 with the 3.11 release, which included 32-bit file management and more networking support.

Then came an almost three year wait for Windows 95, which, as a 32-bit operating system in its own right, can exist without MS-DOS. It is the first 'non-specialist' operating system to make full use of the 32-bit features of the current range of Intel processor chips. Microsoft have also put a lot of effort into this system to make it compatible with almost all existing Windows and MS-DOS based applications. This was obviously necessary, but it has meant that parts of Windows 95 are still only 16-bit in operation.

What about the future? As old PCs are scrapped and the World's population of machines becomes more Pentium processor (and higher) based, and is fitted with larger amounts of memory, we are sure that Windows 95 will be combined with Windows NT to produce one 'all-powerful' full 32-bit operating system.

# ABOUT THIS BOOK

*Windows 95 Explained* was written to help both the beginner and those moving from older versions of Windows. The material in the book is presented on the "what you need to know first, appears first" basis, although you don't have to start at the beginning and go right through to the end. The more experienced user can start from any section, as they have been designed to be self contained.

Windows 95 is a 32-bit operating system with a Graphical User Interface (GUI) front end, and includes built in accessories like a text editor, paint program and many other multi-media, networking and electronic communication features, most of which are examined in this book. Getting to grips with Windows 95, as described, will also reduce the learning curve when it comes to using other Windows application packages.

For example, once you have installed your printers and learned how to switch between them and print from them, you should never again have any difficulty printing from any Windows program. Also, learning to manipulate text and graphics in WordPad and Paint will lay very strong foundations on which to build expertise when you need to master a fully blown word processor with strong elements of desktop publishing.

Windows 95 comes with an updated version of MS-DOS, which is mainly included so that you can run DOS based application programs. If, however, you enjoy using the command line to enter instructions, you still can. We outline the process and cover the main changes to MS-DOS, but we have not attempted to cover the subject fully. If you don't work that way already, you certainly should not start now.

The book was written with the busy person in mind. You don't need to read many hundreds of large format pages to find out most of what there is to know about the subject, when a few pages can get you going quite adequately! It is hoped that with the help of this small book, you will be able to get the most out of your computer, when using Windows 95, in terms of efficiency and productivity, and that you will be able to do it in the shortest, most effective and enjoyable way.

# ABOUT THE AUTHORS

**Phil Oliver** graduated in Mining Engineering at Camborne School of Mines in 1967 and since then has specialised in most aspects of surface mining technology, with a particular emphasis on computer related techniques. He has worked in Guyana, Canada, several Middle Eastern countries, South Africa and the United Kingdom, on such diverse projects as: the planning and management of bauxite, iron, gold and coal mines; rock excavation contracting in the UK; international mining equipment sales and technical back up and international mine consulting for a major mining house in South Africa. In 1988 he took up a lecturing position at Camborne School of Mines (part of Exeter University) in Surface Mining and Management.

**Noel Kantaris** graduated in Electrical Engineering at Bristol University and after spending three years in the Electronics Industry in London, took up a Tutorship in Physics at the University of Queensland. Research interests in Ionospheric Physics, led to the degrees of M.E. in Electronics and Ph.D. in Physics. On return to the UK, he took up a Post-Doctoral Research Fellowship in Radio Physics at the University of Leicester, and then in 1973 a lecturing position in Engineering at the Camborne School of Mines, Cornwall, (part of Exeter University), where since 1978 he has also assumed the responsibility for the Computing Department.

# TRADEMARKS

# ACKNOWLEDGEMENTS

We would like to thank the staff of both Microsoft and Text 100 in the UK, for their valuable help and the generous provision of software for the preparation of this book. We would also like to thank colleagues at the Camborne School of Mines for their helpful suggestions which assisted us in the writing of this book.

# CONTENTS

# 1. PACKAGE OVERVIEW

At long last, after all the wait and all the amazing media hype, Microsoft's replacement for both DOS and Windows 3.x has arrived. After using the full version of Windows 95 for several weeks we have had no real problems and are, to say the least, very happy with it. All our regular programs work, and some of them even go a little faster. The interface looks good and, after the first couple of hours, was easy to come to terms with. Life should be fun, and with Windows 95 using your PC can be a lot more fun. On the down side, our old utility and virus protection software was not compatible and has had to be scrapped. Hopefully, though, we won't need to replace most of it as the new Windows is fairly self sufficient in this respect.

Windows 95 is a graphical interface program, which not only acts as a graphical front end to the Disc Operating System (DOS), as in previous versions, but actually replaces it, and simplifies all the operating system functions. Instead of typing commands at the DOS   C:\> prompt, you now click your mouse on an icon, a folder, an item on a menu system or a colourful bar. Its operating environment is now very similar to that of a Macintosh, with the actual desktop being 'live'. Files, folders, programs and devices, like the printer, can now be placed straight on the desktop, which makes an enormous difference to the way you work, as we will see.

You can still use a DOS prompt, either in a window or full screen, but it is now there simply to let you use programs that were not written with Windows in mind. As you have probably noticed over the last few years, these are becoming more and more unusual. In fact we found that existing DOS programs actually run far better under Windows 95 than they ever did under the previous versions of Windows, as their environment is now much more controllable.

## Some Features New to Windows

A **redesigned graphical interface** that's much simpler to use, with a **Start** button that is always visible and is used for opening programs, file management, system maintenance, and more.

A **Taskbar** makes switching between multiple programs simple. Each time you start a program, a button for it is placed on the Taskbar. When you want to use any program, just click its button.

**Plug and Play** can free you from having to manually set up hardware devices. Windows 95 detects and configures Plug and Play compatible devices automatically. It still works with the hardware and software you already have, so you can get the most from your current applications for the MS-DOS and Windows operating systems.

**Long filenames** make it easy to find what you're looking for. Names can be up to 255 characters.

Windows 95, like Windows NT, is a **32-bit operating system**. This means that the program code of applications running on it can be based on 32-bit numbers (occupying four bytes of memory), rather than the two bytes used by the 16-bit code of DOS or Windows 3.x programs. The ability to handle data in units twice the size, gives the advantage that accessing memory is much faster and more efficient. This 32-bit architecture gives better overall performance and reliability in all areas, especially those of printing, multimedia and networking.

Windows 95 supports true **multi-tasking**, (the ability to run several programs at the same time), as well as multi-threading (the ability to perform several tasks at the same time within one application program). To get full use of these features however your software needs to be written in the new 32-bit format.

**Explorer** gives a graphical view of everything on your computer and makes your system easy to navigate.

**Wizards** to assist with common tasks, and a much more powerful **Help** system. Mind you, with the minimal amount of paper documentation, these are essential.

Faster, smoother **built-in video** makes Windows 95 ideal for multimedia programs and games.

Mouse **right-clicking** on any object will now open a relevant menu, including access to a properties tab folder.

## New Programs and Accessories

As well as a completely different desktop, Windows 95 includes many new and useful programs and accessories, many of them geared to multi-media and network operation, the main ones being:

**WordPad**, a new text editor that you can use to create and modify documents. It has a toolbar for quick access to common tasks and a full range of fonts to use.

**Paint** replaces Paintbrush from Windows 3.x and contains many new features, including movable tool and colour boxes, and print preview.

**Microsoft Exchange** provides a universal in-box that you can use to send and receive e-mail, or organise, access, and share information, such as faxes or items from online services.

**Microsoft Fax** lets you send and receive faxes directly from within Windows.

**The Microsoft Network** (MSN) allows you to easily connect to the Internet, the vaunted 'information super-highway', where you can download thousands of useful files and programs; and some that are 'not so useful'!

**Phone Dialer** lets you make telephone calls from your computer with a modem or another Windows telephony device. You can store a list of phone numbers which you can access quickly.

**File Transfer,** which requires a modem that supports VoiceView, lets you send a file to someone while you are talking to them on the phone.

**HyperTerminal** replaces Terminal from Windows 3.x and lets you easily connect to a remote computer, bulletin board, or other online service.

**Briefcase** helps to keep your files up-to-date when you use two computers, such as your office computer and your portable computer.

**Media Player** plays audio, video, or animation files, and lets you control the settings for multimedia hardware devices, but you need a sound card for this.

**CD Player** lets you play and control an audio CD in a CD-ROM drive on your computer. Also, with **AutoPlay**, an audio CD, or an AutoPlay CD-ROM, will start playing as soon as you place it into the CD-ROM drive.

**Sound Recorder** allows you to record, play, and edit sound files, if you have a sound card and speakers installed on your computer. To record live sound, you also need a microphone.

**Volume Control** lets you change the level of sound coming from your computer's speakers, microphone, or CD-ROM drive, as long as you have a sound card in your computer.

The **MS-DOS Prompt** has been enhanced. It has a button bar, you can start Windows-based programs from the command prompt, and you can close an MS-DOS window by clicking the X (Close) button on the title bar.

You no longer need to use the PIF Editor to specify settings for DOS programs, you now modify their 'properties'.

**Disk Defragmenter** optimises your hard discs so that the saved files are arranged efficiently and do not have unused space between them. Your programs should run faster as your files open more quickly.

**ScanDisk** lets you check your hard discs for errors and automatically fix any problems.

**DriveSpace** lets you compress the files on your discs and free up more space.

**Backup** backs up the files on your hard discs to floppy discs, a tape drive, or another networked computer.

**Quick View** lets you preview a document or file, without actually opening its application program.

**Notepad** is still available to write and edit text files smaller than 64K that do not require formatting. Use WordPad for larger files.

## Hardware Requirements

To install Windows 95, Microsoft say you need at least an IBM AT-compatible PC computer equipped with an Intel 80386 processor, 4MB of RAM (Random Access Memory) and 35-45MB of available hard disc space.

Our minimum specification would be a 486DX PC with 8MB of RAM and at least 50MB of spare hard disc space. The more of both types of memory you have the better, as this operating system is very hungry for both. PC manufactures must be rubbing their hands with glee. Windows 95 will cause many, many, old machines to be scrapped, especially when new software is developed only in 32-bit format to run on Windows 95 or NT. If you have a fast 486, or higher specification PC, we would suggest you think about increasing your on-board RAM, before you start thinking too seriously about a new dream machine.

Although Microsoft have made it easier to operate Windows from the keyboard, the availability of a mouse is a must if you are going to benefit from the program's graphical interface. After all, pointing and clicking a mouse button at an option on the screen is a lot easier than having to learn several different key combinations. Both mouse buttons are now fully utilised.

To be able to use many of Windows features a modem, or fax modem and an audio card with speakers for sound, are also required. You could classify these as optional extras.

## Installing Windows

Installing Windows on your computer system is a very easy process. The installation routine is the best we have seen. We installed an upgrade to Windows 95 from a CD-ROM.

### Preparing your System:

Before you start installing Windows it will pay you to spend a couple of hours on the following housekeeping tasks.

- Go through your whole system with a fine tooth comb and remove any programs, data files or program configuration files that are not absolutely essential. With the advent of CD-ROMS especially, it is too easy these days to get your system in a real mess.

- If you can, defragment your hard disc(s), to make as much contiguous space available for the new system as possible.

- Check your system for viruses, either with MSAV for DOS 6 users, or a proprietary program, such as Norton AntiVirus. Make sure that you disable your antivirus software before carrying on.

- Turn off any screen savers or other memory resident programs.

- Make sure you have a floppy disc that will start your PC with your present version of DOS. Also make sure your PC does not prevent start-up from your floppy disc drive. If it does, you will have to explore your PC

6

BIOS set-up options, usually reached by pressing the **F2** key on start up.

**Some Options to Consider** - During the installation you will be asked to choose from several important options, without being made aware of some of the implications of your choices.

Unless you have enormous amounts of spare hard disc space and time, we suggest you opt to have Windows 95 install in the same directory as your previous version of Windows. If you don't, you will have to re-install all your existing Windows application programs, before being able to run them in Windows 95.

We suggest you definitely opt to save your existing system files. This will take up about 6MB of valuable hard disc space, but will enable you to return your system to the old set-up if things start going wrong.

When asked, let the Setup program make a new floppy start up disc, **but not on top of your old system one!**

## The Installation:

To start installation from DOS, insert the Windows 95 CD-ROM, or place the Setup Disc 1 into drive A:, log onto the correct drive and type the command

```
Setup
```

If you are upgrading from a previous version of Windows, you should carry out this operation with Windows running, in the text box opened with the **File**, **Run** Program Manager menu command.

The whole installation procedure is fairly intuitive but we will step through the main parts of our installation. If you make different selections, or are starting with the full installation from DOS, rather than a Windows upgrade, your sequence may not be exactly the same, but that should not create too many problems.

An initial Welcome screen opens and a routine check is made of your system. If you do not have enough hard disc space you will be told very early on.

If any problems are found with your hard disc(s) you will be instructed to exit the installation and run the program SCANDISK to check and fix your drive(s). This can be very time consuming, but is essential we assure you.

To do this, use the command

```
f:\win95\scandisk.exe /all
```

for a CD-ROM installation with F: being the CD-ROM drive. With a disc installation, place Setup Disc 1 into the A: drive and use the command

```
a:\scandisk.exe /all
```

Let SCANDISK fix any errors it finds. On ours it found 3 disc errors that we were unaware of! You then start again!

A 'Setup Wizard' guides you through the rest of the installation. If you haven't encountered Wizards before, they are Microsoft's way of semi-automating procedures, and are used extensively in their latest Windows software.

Read and accept the licence agreement, as long as you are installing a legal copy of the program, of course.

You have probably worked out by now that pressing the **Next** button on a screen moves you one step forward!

As mentioned previously, we suggest you install in the same directory as your old version of Windows, and opt to save your existing system files. You can always delete them later when you are up and running.

We selected a **Typical** setup which installs standard options with default settings, but if you are installing to a portable PC you can select **Portable**. If your disc space is very limited you could try **Compact** to install a cut-down version. Use the **Custom** option if you know the way round your system.

Enter, or confirm, your name and company details. We were then asked to enter a 10 digit key number 'from the back of the CD-ROM' case. Our initial demo copy did not have such a number so we carried on regardless, without any apparent problems. We haven't been asked since.

If you are connected to the Internet, or have e-mail facilities, make suitable selections on the next screens, otherwise press **Next** and think about getting connected!

You are then asked to select the Windows components you want installed. Don't worry at this stage, if you omit anything you can always add it at a later date.

A start-up disc is then made and all the necessary files are copied to your hard disc(s).

If all is well, and quite a while later, you will be asked to remove any discs from your floppy drives and to press **Finish** to re-start your computer. This is the nail biting time, it seems to take forever for the PC to actually start up again.

When it finally does, you are into the last stages of the installation. You may be asked to enter a user name and password. This is so that if several people use your PC each can maintain his/her own setup. Quite clever, but if this is not necessary for you, leave the password text box blank. The program then works its way through the final steps. It builds the Control Panel, places your application programs, and some of its own, on the Start Menu, 'writes' the Windows Help and sorts out the DOS program settings.

The last item on the list gives you a first chance to see the superb standard of presentation of Windows 95.

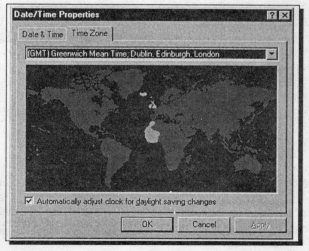

You are asked to set your time zone, followed by the actual date and time. To change your time zone, click the down arrow at the right end of the list box, as shown on the previous page. Select GMT from the opened list, unless of course you are reading this in another part of the World. Make sure the small box next to the **Automatically adjust clock for daylight saving changes** is selected, then click the 'Date & Time' tab to open the other dialogue box similar to that shown below.

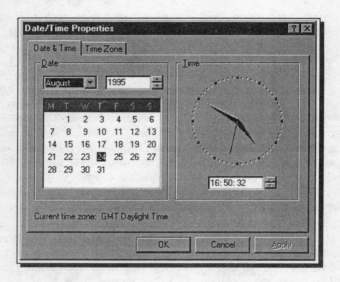

If necessary, make changes to the date and time settings, and click on **Close** to complete the installation process.

It took us the best part of an hour to install Windows 95, but patience paid off in the end. Our opening screen is shown on the facing page, but depending on your settings and your PC, yours may not look exactly the same.

## Welcome to Windows 95

While the Welcome box shown is open, take a few minutes to use its facilities. If you installed from a CD-ROM you should be able to click on the **Windows Tour** button to get a quick

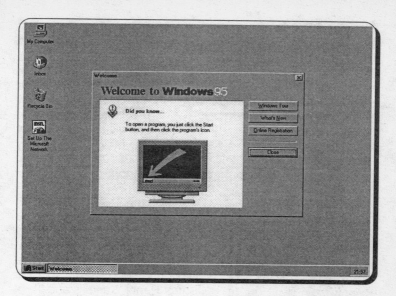

overview of the new version. It needs quite a bit of memory to run though.

The **What's New** button opens a series of answers to some common questions about how Windows has changed.

**Online Registration** is only of use if you have a modem connected. It opens a Wizard to step you through the procedure of registering your new software with Microsoft. How's that for progress, but what other information is sent at the same time we do not know. If you have any illegal copies of Microsoft software on your PC, beware!

Click the **Close** button when you have finished, to be left with the new Windows' desktop, which initially consists of a coloured background with several icons down the left side, a bar across the bottom with a **START** button in the left corner and probably a digital clock in the right corner. What icons appear will depend on your system, but the two that will always be there are **My Computer** and the **Recycle Bin**. What names! The first gives visual access to your PC system and the other is a trash can which holds files deleted from your hard disc(s), until you 'empty' it. Until you get used to this, you may find your hard disc space filling up rather faster than you expect.

## The START Button

This button is the key to many of Windows' operations, which

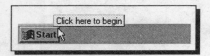

is why it formed the focus of the launch advertising campaign. If you move the mouse pointer over the button a help flag opens giving you a hint of its function, as shown here. These yellow messages actually form the first level of Help in Windows 95. Try moving the pointer over the other features of the desktop.

Clicking the START button opens the default Start menu shown here. This gives access to **Programs** that you can open, to the **Documents** you have most recently used, to the Control Panel, printers and Task bar **Settings**, to a much improved file and (other PC) **Find**er, to the Windows 95 new **Help** system and to a **Run** box in which you can open a program, folder or a document. The last item even remembers your previous commands to make life a little easier.

### Opening and Exiting Windows 95:

As we saw, after the setup procedure, Windows starts up on its own when you switch your PC on. To start up to a DOS prompt, you must press the F8 key when the screen message 'Starting Windows 95' appears (soon after you switch on your PC) and choose Command Prompt Only.

To leave Windows, you click the START button, followed by **Shut Down**. On our machine, this opens the dialogue box shown opposite. You might have an extra option if you share your PC with other users.

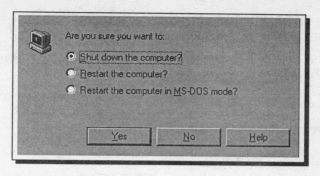

Selecting the default option, **Shut down the computer?**
exits all the open programs, carries out any file saves you
require and then tells you when it is safe to switch off. This is
the only way you should end a session. Never just switch off
your PC.

The other options are self explanatory. **Restart the**
**computer?** clears memory settings, etc., and restarts
Windows, whereas **Restart the computer in MS-DOS**
**mode?** starts up with just a DOS prompt. This might be
necessary for an older program written for DOS. In fact
Windows automates this procedure when it encounters such
a recalcitrant program. **Close all programs and log on as a**
**different user?**, does just that, but only if your PC is set up
for multi-users, each with their own password. Ours isn't, so
that option is not shown.


## Uninstalling Windows 95

In the Setup procedure, as we saw earlier, you have the
option of saving your system files so that you can uninstall
Windows 95 later. You will not see this Setup option if you
are upgrading over an earlier version of Windows 95, or if
you are installing to a new directory, or your version of
MS-DOS is earlier than 5.0.

In the unlikely event that you have serious problems, or
you prefer your older setup, as long as you have saved your
system files, you can uninstall Windows 95 and restore your
computer to its previous versions of MS-DOS and Windows,
as follows:

1    Click the START button, point to **Settings**, and then click Control Panel.
2    Double-click the **Add/Remove Programs** icon.
3    On the **Install/Uninstall** tab, click **Windows 95**, and then click **Add/Remove**.

The uninstall program needs to shut down Windows 95. If there is a problem with this on your PC, restart your computer and press F8 when you see the message 'Starting Windows 95'. Then choose Command Prompt Only, and run UNINSTAL from the command prompt.

If you are having problems starting Windows 95, use the startup disc, created during the installation, to start your computer, and then run UNINSTAL from the startup disc.

## Removing Old System Files:

Once you are happy that Windows 95 is running well on your system you can remove the uninstall files to free up between 6 to 9 MB of hard disc space; to do this carry out the following procedure:

1    Click the START button, point to **Settings**, and then click Control Panel.
2    Double-click the **Add/Remove Programs** icon.
3    On the Install/Uninstall tab, click **Old Windows 3.x and MS-DOS System Files**, then click **Add/Remove** again.

Remember that once you have done this you will no longer be able to uninstall Windows 95.

To save even more hard disc space you could also delete the remaining files in your old DOS directory. Be careful though as some of these may prove useful in the future. Make sure you keep the files for all your back up programs. The Windows 95 Backup does not restore files made with earlier versions.

# 2. WORKING WITH WINDOWS 95

## The Windows Desktop

The look and feel of Windows has been improved to make it easier and faster for you to get your work done. When you start Windows, the large area you see is called the desktop. You can customise the desktop by adding shortcuts to your favourite programs, documents, and printers, and by changing its look to fit your mood and personality.

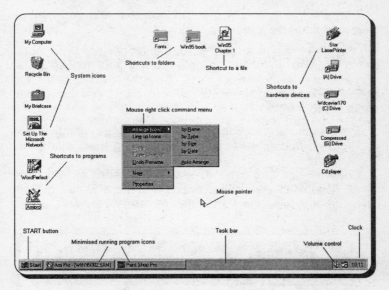

Our example above, is now a little different from that of the previous chapter. We have changed the background colour to white, to make the screen dumps for the book a little clearer, and added quite a few icons.

## Desktop Icons:

The system icons above are:

**My Computer** - double-click this to graphically browse through all your files and folders.
**Recycle Bin** - a waste basket for deleted files and folders.

15

**My Briefcase** - used to help maintain the same file sets on two different computers.
**Set up the Microsoft Network** - used to set up access to Microsoft's new World-wide network.

If your computer is attached to a network you will also have the following icons installed for you:

**Network Neighbourhood** - double-click this to browse through the computers in your local work group and on your entire network.
**Inbox** - this is the in and out box that lets you control e-mail and faxes, etc.

All the other icons shown in our example are 'shortcuts' which point to an object, double-clicking your mouse on a shortcut opens the object itself. See the next chapter for details on creating shortcuts of your own. You can have shortcuts to:

**Programs** (applications) - these replace Windows 3.x Program Manager items. Double-clicking them starts the program.
**Folders** - as sub-directories are now called in Windows 95. Double-clicking them opens a window showing their contents, (documents and other folders) as shown below.

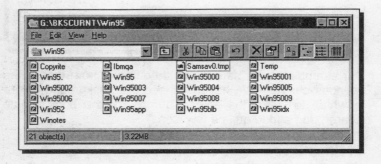

**Documents** (files) - Double-clicking a shortcut to a document opens the document and the program it was produced by, so you can just carry on working with it.

**Devices** - such as disc drives and printers. Double-clicking will activate the device, or open a window onto its contents. You can drag a document icon (by mouse clicking on it and moving the pointer with the left mouse button depressed) onto a printer shortcut to print the document.

## The Taskbar:

At the bottom of the desktop screen is the Taskbar. It contains the START button, which as we shall soon see, can be used to quickly start a program, or to find a file, and it is also the fastest way to get Help.

When you open a program, or a window, a button for it is placed on the Taskbar. You can click your mouse on this button to make this the active program, or window. So, no matter how cluttered your screen is, you can always see what windows you have open and quickly switch between them. As more buttons are placed on the Taskbar their size shrinks, as shown below.

If you need to see more details on a truncated button, hold the mouse pointer over it. Alternatively, you can drag the top of the bar up and have multiple rows of buttons, as shown below. This reduces the area of the desktop though.

The Taskbar also shows the current time, and, when they are installed, icon controls for sound cards, modems and other

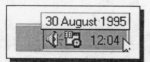

features, as shown here. Moving the mouse pointer over the clock will display the date. Double-clicking the clock, opens the Date/Time Properties box,

17

seen in Chapter 1, so that you can make changes, if necessary.

Clicking your mouse on the 'speaker' icon, opens the Volume slider shown on the right. With this, you can easily and quickly adjust the volume coming from your sound card. If you want more complex control of sound output see the section on the CD Player in Chapter 6.

## Using a Mouse

As with all graphical based programs, using a mouse makes most operations easier and more fun to carry out. Windows 95 has several different mouse pointers, some illustrated below, which it uses for its various functions. When the program is initially started up the first you will see is the hourglass, which tells you to wait. This turns into an upward pointing hollow arrow for most operations, and a large I-beam when the pointer is over a text entry or editing area.

Often the pointer appears over a window as an arrow with an hourglass attached, this means you cannot work with that window until some current action is completed. You will be able to action other windows, however.

With Windows 95 you can, in fact, customise all your mouse pointers from the Control Panel.

**Mouse Pointers:**

 The hourglass which displays when you are waiting while Windows starts up.

 The arrow which appears when the pointer is placed over the desktop, menus, scrolling bars, and buttons, etc.

I The I-beam which appears in normal text areas of windows.

✥ The large 4-headed arrow which appears after choosing the **Control, Move/Size** command(s) for moving or sizing windows.

18

Double arrows which appear when over the border of a window, used to drag the side and alter the size of the window.

 The Help hand which appears in the help windows, and is used to access 'hypertext' type links.

 The 'What's this?' pointer which appears on the screen after you click the ? button on the right end of the title bar of some windows. Pointing to an object in the window and clicking opens a Help topic.

 The 'No go' pointer which tells you that you cannot perform the current function here.

 The application busy pointer. Try actioning another window!

## Mouse Right Clicking:

You can use your right mouse button to click any object and see a shortcut menu, containing common commands applicable to the item clicked. For example, try clicking an

 icon with your right mouse button. We didn't want the icon for setting up the network, so we right-clicked it here.

As you can see, we could carry out 9 different operations from the opened menu. Pressing **Delete** moves it from the desktop to the Recycle Bin, but only after a warning message is shown.

Try, as another example, right clicking the mouse button anywhere on the desktop. This should open the menu shown on Page 15, which also shows the options available for arranging icons on the desktop. To adjust other desktop settings, such as colour or background,

19

you click **Properties**. When you want to view or change information about any object, such as a document, program, folder, disc drive, or printer, you do it from its properties sheet, or dialogue box. This is one of Windows 95's strong new control features.

**Keyboard Shortcuts:**
As well as using the mouse, Windows now allows you to carry out most tasks from the keyboard. Full details of possible keyboard actions are given in Appendix A.

## Running a Program

Users of previous versions of Windows are probably suffering withdrawal symptoms by now, as there are no Program Manager icons to double-click, to open programs. As we saw, you can place icons on the desktop for this, but at the moment we don't know how to. The key, at this stage, is clicking the START button.

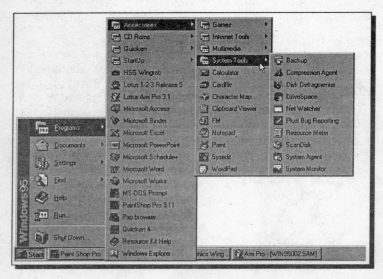

This opens the Start menu, shown on the left above. Holding the pointer over the **Programs** option will open a cascading menu, which initially has the same options as the original

Program Manager of your previous Windows version. Unless, of course, your PC did not have Windows installed.

Moving the pointer over menu items with a '➤' character on their right, opens yet another level of cascading menus. To open, or run, a program you simply click on its entry on one of these menus. You may need to practice a little with your mouse as the menus disappear if you move off them.

You can access the START menu system without using a mouse, by pressing the keyboard combination <Ctrl+Esc>. (Press the Escape key while the Control key is pressed). You then use the arrow keys to move the highlight around the menus and press the <Enter> key when the option you want is selected. To close the menu system, keep pressing the <Esc> key until all the menus have closed, or click the mouse with the pointer somewhere else on the desktop.

If you want to know how to change any of the menu options, you could read ahead to the Taskbar Menus section of Chapter 4.

As an example, open the menu system, locate the WordPad item shown here, and click on it. This will open the new Windows built-in word processor into its own window, as shown below, and place an icon on the Taskbar.

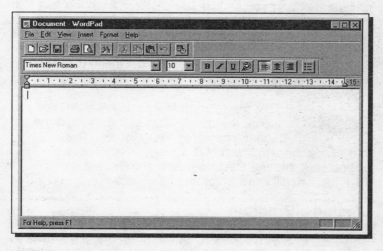

We will look at this utility a little later on.

## Opening a Document:

 There are usually at least two ways of opening documents from within Windows applications. Clicking the Open icon shown here, or with the **File**, **Open** menu command. Both open a new Windows 95 dialogue box with, in this case, Windows being the current directory, as shown below.

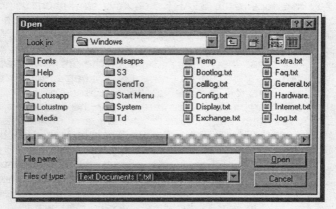

Make sure that Text Documents [*.txt] is selected in the **Files of type** box and you should see a selection of the text files that Microsoft provide with the program. Select the file Tips.txt and click the **Open** button. You can now read or edit the file. In fact we strongly recommend that you browse through all these text files. Some may not mean very much to you, but some, especially Tips.txt are full of useful information.

 To read the document more easily, you can click the middle icon of the three in the top right corner of the window. This maximises the window to full screen, but changes as you click it to the Restore button shown here on the right. You click this to return to a window.

## Closing a Program

 The new way to close a program (or a window) is to click the X icon, shown here. If you are used to a previous version of Windows you should be very careful. This new close button has replaced the previous maximise button. We have fallen foul of this change at least once and deleted a document when we didn't mean to. You have been warned.

## Re-opening Documents
A very useful new feature is the ability to very quickly open one of the documents you have recently been working with.

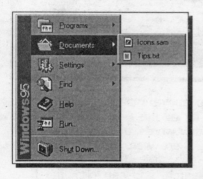

The **Documents** option on the START menu, lists the 15 most recent files you have accessed. Clicking one of these, opens the document as well as the application that it was created in.

Unfortunately, not all files that are opened from inside programs seem to register on this list. We will touch on the other ways of opening programs in Windows later.

To clear the document list, click **Settings** on the START menu, select the **Taskbar** option and click the Start Menu Programs tab of the dialogue box that opens. Finally, click the **Clear** button as shown here.

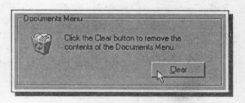

## Finding a File
Unless you are super efficient, you will often want to access a file, or document, but not be able to remember its name, or where you put it. Windows 95 has a very powerful facility for coping with such situations.

To access it, select **Find** from the START menu, and if you have a choice, select **Files or Folders...**, which opens the Find:All Files dialogue box.

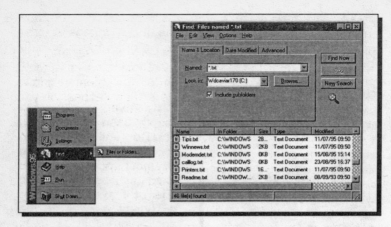

The composite screen dump above shows the open menu and the result of searching for all the files on our C: drive which fit the mask '*.txt'. In other words, all files that end with the suffix '.txt'. In our case there were 46 of them, time indeed for a clear out!

If you want to refine a search, you can click the Date Modified or Advanced tabs of the Find dialogue box. To set a folder where the search should begin, click **Browse**. When all the search criteria are entered, click **Find Now**.

Finding a list of files is not much use unless you can do something with it. Right clicking on one of the located files opens a command menu, which should be similar to that alongside. Plenty of actions are possible here.

To save the results of a search along with the search criteria, select **Save Results** from the **Options** menu.

An icon, like the one shown here, is placed on your desktop. Double-clicking this icon will repeat the search at any time in the future. To save cluttering up your desktop you could place this icon in a special folder, maybe with other search patterns, or other utilities.

## Parts of a Window

It is perhaps worth spending some time looking at the various parts that make up a window, where we use the word 'Windows' to refer to the whole environment, while 'window', or 'windows' refers to application or document windows. There are several types of windows that can appear on your screen; some created by Windows itself, and other 'applications' windows which contain running applications, and also 'document' windows. The latter appear with programs that can open more than one document, but they share the application window's menu and other features.

Each application, and some documents you choose to work with, open and use separate windows to run in. We have used a typical window to illustrate its various parts. Although every window has some common elements, not all windows will use all of these elements.

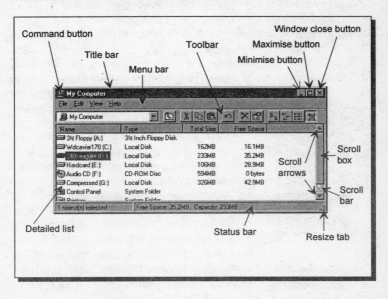

This window is easily opened by double-clicking the 'My Computer' desktop icon. It displays a solid 'Title bar', indicating that it is the active applications window. Although multiple windows can be displayed simultaneously, you can

25

only work in the active window (usually displayed at the top). Title bars of non-active windows appear a lighter shade than that of the active one.

A window is subdivided into several areas which have the following functions:

| Area | Function |
|---|---|
| Command button | Clicking on this program icon button, located in the upper-left corner of each window, displays the pull-down Control menu which can be used to control the window. It includes commands for restoring, maximising, minimising, moving, sizing, and closing the window. |
| Title bar | The bar at the top of a window. The actual title depends on the type of Windows application. |
| Menu bar | The bar below the title bar which allows you to choose from several menu options. Clicking on a menu item displays the pull-down menu associated with that item. The specific options listed in the Menu bar depend on the application running in the window. |
| Minimise button | The button you point to and click to reduce an application to an icon on the Taskbar. |
| Maximise button | The button you point to and click to fill the screen with the active window. When that happens, the Maximise button changes to a Restore button (page 22) which can be used to restore the window to its former size |
| Close button | The new X button that you click to close the window. |
| Toolbar | A bar of icons that you click to carry out some of the more common actions, like cutting, copying, etc. |

| Scroll bars | If the contents of a window will not fit in it, scroll bars are added to the right and/or the bottom of the window. Clicking on these bars allows you to see the window contents that are not visible. |
| --- | --- |
| Scroll arrows | The arrowheads at each end of a scroll bar which you can click to scroll the screen up and down one line, or left and right one character, at a time. |
| Status bar | The bar at the bottom of a window in which the current status or the present process is displayed. |
| Resize tab | Drag on this tab with your mouse pointer to resize the window. |

## The Menu Bar Options:

Each window's menu bar option has associated with it a pull-down sub-menu. To this menu, either use the mouse to point to an option, or press the <Alt> key, which causes the first option of the menu (in this case **File**) to be highlighted, then use the arrow keys to highlight any of the options in the menu. Pressing either the <Enter> key, or the left mouse button, reveals the pull-down sub-menu of the highlighted menu option. The sub-menu of the **File** option of the maximised My Computer window, is shown below.

Menu options can also be activated directly by pressing the <Alt> key followed by the underlined letter of the required option. Thus pressing **<Alt+F>**, also opens the sub-menu of **File**.

You can use the up and down arrow keys to move the highlighted bar up and down a sub-menu, or the right and left arrow keys to move along the options in the menu bar. Pressing the <Enter> key selects the highlighted option or executes the highlighted command. Pressing the

27

<Esc> key once, closes the pull-down sub-menu, while pressing the <Esc> key for a second time, closes the menu system.

Menu items common to most windows are:

**File**     Produces a pull-down menu of file and disc related tasks, such as **Open**ing a file, opening the **Explore**r, **Find**ing a file, **Format**ting the selected disc drive, **Create** a **shortcut** to, **Delete**, **Rename** or open the **Properties** of, the selected item, and finally to **Close** the window.

**Edit**        Gives access to the common editing tasks which can be carried out on the selected item.

**View**       Options to control the appearance of the window. The **Toolbar** and **Status bar** options set whether these features are displayed. A checkmark against either, sets it on. Selecting the option once more, removes the checkmark and toggles the option off.

Most of Windows 95 system windows let you display their contents in one of 4 ways, with **Large Icons**, **Small icons**, as a plain **List**, or as a **Detail**ed list. There are options to **Arrange Icons** in various ways, or to **Auto Arrange** them (in which case they 'jump around' the window as you re-size it). **Refresh**, re-displays the window showing any changes made, and **Options** opens a dialogue box giving you even more control over the displayed window.

**Help**       Activates the help window, or opens a window giving basic details of the system and the available resources.

## Toolbars:

Most Windows 95 system windows are now fully equipped with a Toolbar option, as shown below. These have even been extended to DOS Prompt windows.

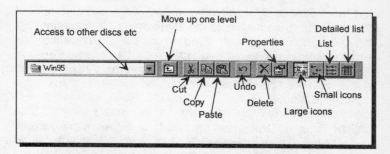

If the Toolbar is not showing when a window is opened, you simply open the **View** menu and select the **Toolbar** option. This places a tick '√' character against the option. Selecting it again, in the future, will toggle the option off.

## Dialogue Boxes:

Three periods after a sub-menu option or command, means that a dialogue box will open when the option or command is selected. A dialogue box is used for the insertion of additional information, such as the name of a file, or to change settings.

To see a dialogue box, open the WordPad, as described earlier, and action the **File**, **Page Setup** menu command. The dialogue box, shown here, appears on the screen.

You usually move round a dialogue box with the mouse, but the <Tab> key can be used to move the highlight from one field to the next, (<Shift+Tab> moves the cursor backwards) or alternatively you can move directly to a desired field by holding the <Alt> key down and pressing the underlined letter in the field name. Within a group of options you can use the arrow keys to move from one option to another. Having selected an option or typed in information, you must press a command button such as the **OK** or **Cancel** button, or choose from additional options. To select the **OK** button with the mouse, simply point and click, while with the keyboard, you must first press the <Tab> key until the dotted rectangle, called the focus, moves to the required button, and then press the <Enter> key.

Some dialogue boxes contain List boxes which show a column of available choices. If there are more choices than can be seen in the area provided, use the scroll bars to reveal them. To select a single item from a List box, either double-click the item, or use the arrow keys to highlight the item and press <Enter>. Dialogue boxes may contain Option buttons with a list of mutually exclusive items. The default choice is marked with a black dot against its name, while unavailable options are dimmed. Another type of dialogue box option is the Check box which offers a list of features you can switch on or off. Selected options show a tick in the box against the option name.

If you can't work out the function of something in a dialogue box there are two quick ways of getting context sensitive help. Clicking the **?** button, next to the Close button in the top right corner of the box, will add a question mark to the pointer. Click this on the unknown item and an explanation window will open up.

Alternatively, right clicking the mouse on an option, opens the **What's This?** button, as shown here. Selecting this button will open the same text window as described above.

To cancel a dialogue box, either press the **Cancel** button, or press the <Esc> key enough times, to close the dialogue box and then the menu system.

## Properties Sheets:

Another type of dialogue box, new to Windows 95, is the tabbed property settings sheet, used for every Windows object. These are easily opened by selecting the **Properties** option from an object's right click menu.

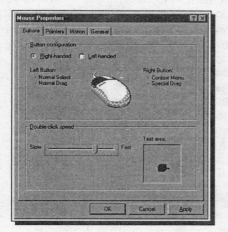

The Mouse Properties sheet shown here was opened in a different way, by opening the START menu and selecting **Settings**, **Control Panel** and then double-clicking on the Mouse option.

Instead of one big box with all the options crammed on, the sheet has a set of tabs across the top, which open three other sheets of related settings. If you look through these you will find all sorts of other ways Windows lets you control settings.

## Manipulating Windows

Windows 95, by definition, allows the display of multiple system and application windows on the screen. To effectively use the program you must be able to manipulate these windows, which may involve selecting which is to be the active one, by moving them so that you can see all the relevant parts of an application, by changing their size and maybe the layout of those that are open.

In the following few pages methods are given for both a mouse and using the keyboard. You can obviously ignore whichever method you don't want to use.

## Changing the Active Window:

There are several ways to make a window the active one. If you can see part of it on the desktop area, simply point to it and click the left mouse button.

Holding the <Alt> key down and pressing the <Tab> key will open a pop-up box showing the icons of all open windows. This will stay visible as long as the <Alt> key is held down. Pressing the <Tab> key moves the highlight through this listing and when the icon you want is selected, releasing the <Alt> key will make that the active window. This was the fastest way to move between applications in the previous versions of Windows, but research showed that not many users seemed to know about it.

To solve this, a new way, unique to Windows 95, uses the fact that whenever a window is open its icon is placed on the Taskbar, and is thus usually visible at all times. Simply click this Taskbar icon to make that window active and bring it to the top. This really is a great improvement, and has been likened to changing channels on a television set by clicking a controller.

## Moving Windows:

When you have multiple windows or dialogue boxes open on the desktop, you often want to move one to a different part of the screen. This can be done with either the mouse or the keyboard.

To move a window, or an icon, **with the mouse**, point to the title bar or icon and drag it (press the left button and keep it pressed while moving the mouse) until the shadow border

is where you would like it to be. Then release the mouse button to fix it into its new position.

To move a system or application window **with the keyboard**, press <Alt+Spacebar> to open its Control menu as shown here, (or <Alt+-> to open a document window's Control menu). Then, press **m** to select **Move** which causes a four-headed arrow to appear in the title bar and use the arrow keys to move the shadow border of the window to the required place. Press

32

<Enter> to fix the window to its new position or <Esc> to cancel relocation.

## Sizing a Window:

You can also change the size of a window with either the mouse or the keyboard.

To size an active window **with the mouse**, move the window so that the side you want to change is visible, then move the mouse pointer to the edge of the window or a corner so that it changes to a two-headed arrow, then drag this arrow in the direction you want that side or corner to move. Some windows now have a Resize tab in their bottom right corner to make this process easier. Continue dragging until the shadow border is the size you require, then release the mouse button.

To size **with the keyboard**, press either <Alt+Spacebar> or <Alt+–> to reveal the Application Control menu or the Document Control menu, then press **s** to select S̲ize which causes a four-headed arrow to appear. Now, from the keyboard, press the arrow key that corresponds to the edge you want to move, or if a corner, press the two arrow keys (one after the other) corresponding to the particular corner, which causes the pointer to change to a two-headed arrow. Press an appropriate arrow key in the direction you want that side or corner to move and continue to do so until the shadow border is the size you require, then press <Enter> to fix the new window size.

## Minimising and Maximising Windows:

Windows can be minimised into Taskbar icons, to temporarily free desktop space. This can be done by either using the mouse to click at the 'Minimise' button in the upper-right corner of the window, or by pressing <Alt+Spacebar> or <Alt+–> to reveal the Application Control menu or the Document Control menu, and selecting **n** for Mi̲nimize.

To maximise a window so that it fills the entire desktop, either click on the 'maximise' button, or press <Alt+Spacebar> or <Alt+–> to display the Application Control menu or the Document Control menu, and select **x** for Ma̲ximize.

An application which has been minimised or maximised can be returned to its original size and position on the screen by either clicking its Taskbar icon to expand it to a window, or clicking on the 'Restore' button in the upper-right corner of the maximised window to reduce it to its former size. With the keyboard, select **r** for **Restore** from the Control menu.

## Closing a Window

Any window can be closed at any time to save screen space and memory. To close a window **with a mouse**, either double click on its Control menu button (the icon in the upper-left corner of the window title bar), or click its X Close button on the right hand end of the same bar.

**With the keyboard**, either select **c** for **Close** from the window Control menu or use one of the following shortcut commands: <Ctrl+F4> to close a document window, or <Alt+F4> to close a system or application window.

If you have made any changes to a document since the last time you saved it, Windows will warn you with a dialogue box asking confirmation prior to closing it.

## Windows Display Arrangements

Whenever you use Windows, it is inevitable that you will end up with several windows open at any one time. If you want to organise these a little try right-clicking an empty part of the Taskbar, which opens the menu shown here.

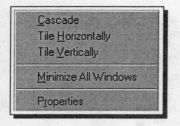

In **Cascade** form all open windows overlap one another, with each newly opened window being located slightly below and to the right of the previous one.

With the two Tile options, windows are displayed adjacent to each other, either Vertically, or Horizontally, depending on your choice. The **Minimize All Windows** choice produces a 'clear' start-up type desktop.

As an illustration, the tile type of display arrangement is shown below with four open windows.

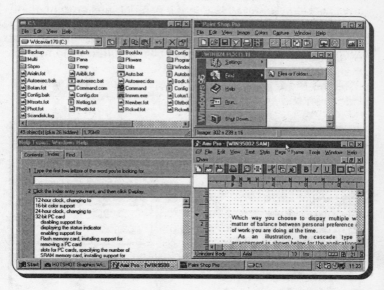

The 'Ami Pro' window (bottom right) is the active one, as shown by the darker title bar and its icon highlighted on the Taskbar.

The same windows arrange themselves automatically in the display form shown below when the Cascade option is selected.

## Using the Help System

On-line Help has been completely revised in Windows 95 and Microsoft seem proud to say that it is much easier to use and to learn. We have some reservations here though. Not only have they cut down on the paper manual information, but they do not include much depth to the standard Help system either. Even the glossary has gone!

Use the Start, **Help** menu command to open the main Help window, shown on the left below.

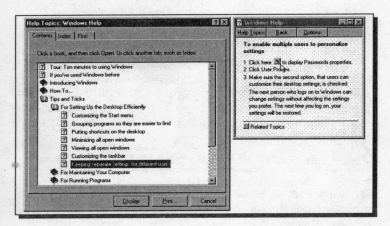

The Contents tab displays top level 'chapters', shown as book icons, which you double-click to open a very short page of text, as shown on the right above .

Some Help topics contain shortcut buttons, like the one shown here, these take you straight to the relevant area of the main program. In the example above, clicking this icon in the Help page would move you straight to the Password properties section.

The Index tab opens an interactive Help index. If you type the first few letters of a word you are shown the available options. Selecting one and clicking the **Display** button opens its page. When you have read it, click the **Help Topics** button to return to the main Help window.

The Find tab gives you access to a very powerful individual word search facility of the Help system.

# 3. DISCS, FOLDERS AND FILES

One of the main functions of any operating system is to control the use of the system's disc drives and the manipulation of the data stored on them. Many users of MS-DOS will be well used to doing this by typing commands (such as Dir, Copy, Move or Delete) at the DOS prompt (such as C:\>) and having to refer to files by first remembering, and then typing in, their actual names. If you mastered this procedure, fine, but many PC users didn't.

Previous versions of Microsoft Windows gave a much easier way of manipulating discs and files with its semi-graphical File Manager.

Windows 95 has maintained, and improved, both these methods, but has also revolutionised the way files, folders and discs can be handled on the PC. In the 'My Computer' facility almost everything can now be done graphically, by clicking and dragging icons between windows, folders and the desktop itself.

## Folders

 In Windows 95, files are organised in folders. These are graphical devices, as shown here, similar to directories in that they can contain files and other folders, but they can also contain icons.

## Working with Files

As we shall see, there are many ways of carrying out most disc and file operations in Windows 95.

Die-hard DOS users should be quite happy carrying out much of their work in an MS-DOS Prompt window. They probably will not need too much help from us, but Chapter 9 may ease the conversion process.

Previous Windows users may prefer to use the Windows Explorer for their disc and file manipulations. This, much beefed-up version of the older File Manager, is described later in the chapter.

New Windows users should definitely start out with 'My Computer', covered next, which Microsoft have spent much time and effort making as intuitive as possible.

## My Computer

My Computer

Double-clicking the My Computer icon on the desktop gives you immediate visual access to all the disc drives in your computer, as well as the Control Panel and the Printers folder. The window opened should look similar to that below. It would obviously only look exactly the same if your computer had the same components as ours.

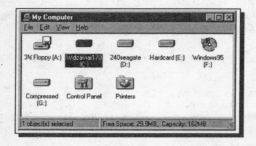

The default settings shown are specially designed so as not to confuse new users. These consist of large icons, no toolbar and each time you double-click an icon a new window opens showing its contents. Icon settings are easy to change, however, from the **View** menu, as shown below.

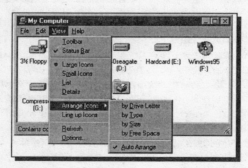

Try changing these settings to see the results. Using the **View**, **Options** command also allows you to control the number of windows opened at a time, which file types are displayed and whether their extensions are shown.

Each drive type has a different icon in the first My Computer window. It will even show you what type of CD is in the CD-ROM drive. In our example it was the Windows 95 CD in our F drive.

To look a little deeper in your system, double-click the icon for your C drive, and in the newly opened window, double-click the folder named 'Windows' to open another window, similar to ours below. If you can't see the folder, you may have to use the scroll bars to move through the contents of the C window. (If you installed Windows 95 on a different drive you should look in that drive, instead of C).

You can see from the title bar above that this is displaying some of the contents of the folder C:\Windows. Folders, on the top row, have the previously described folder icon. All the other icons represent files. If you look carefully, you will see that most of the file names do not show an extension. By default, Windows 95 does not display file extensions. These extensions are used by the program to associate files with the applications that they are used with. If a valid association exists, the application icon is shown in the My Computer window, but if not, the extension is displayed.

Any file displayed without its extension can be opened from a window by double-clicking its icon. If it is a program file, the program will run. If it is a document, it will be opened in a running version of its application program.

To see what program associations are valid on your system use the **View**, **Options** menu command from any My

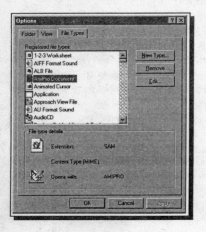

Computer window and click the File Types tab. This will open the dialogue box window shown here.

If you work your way down the list of **Registered file types** you can see the association details in the lower half of the box. Our example shows that an AmiPro document has the file extension .SAM. From this box you can add new associations by clicking the **New Type** button, delete them with the

**Remove** button and change them with the **Edit** button. Without getting too involved at this stage, it is worth spending a few minutes just browsing through the list. It will help you recognise the icons.

## Opening a New Folder:

Before we start manipulating any files we will open a new folder to hold copies of some existing files. It should then be safe to 'play around' with them. If necessary, open a My Computer window showing the C drive contents and right

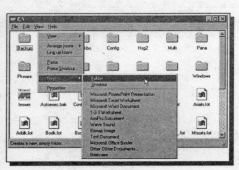

click your mouse on an empty part of the window. This will open the command menu shown on the left. Holding the pointer over **New** will then open the cascade menu. Clicking the pointer on the **Folder** option will

40

place a new, but blue, folder in the window, as shown here on the left. Its temporary name is highlighted ready for you to type its proper name. Type **Practice folder**

into the name slot and press the <Enter> key. Its as easy as that to create and name a folder. At any time in the future you can rename it by clicking its existing name and typing in the new one. This works for files too. Now double-click the new icon to open the folder.

## Long Filenames:
The above also demonstrates that with Windows 95 you are not restricted to the old DOS 8.3 character (filename. extension) convention. You can now give any name to a file, or to a folder; you are not limited to eight characters with a three-character extension. You can also use spaces, as we did above. Beware though, only programs written for Windows 95 will recognise any long file names.

## Selecting Files and Folders:
If you have worked through the chapter so far, you should have several open windows on the desktop. Arrange the new Practice folder window alongside that showing the contents of the C drive as shown below.

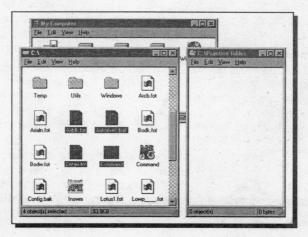

41

So far we have selected one window object by clicking it with the left mouse button. To select several objects, or icons, you have two options. If they form a rectangle, as on the previous page, click one corner, then with the <Shift> key depressed, click the opposite corner. To select random objects hold the <Ctrl> key down and click them, one by one. To select all the files and folders in a window use the **Edit**, **Select All** menu command, or the keyboard shortcut <Ctrl+A>. To cancel a selection, you just click the pointer somewhere else in the window.

## Copying Files and Folders:

As usual there are several ways to copy selected icons from one window to another.

**Using the menu** of the source window (in our case from the C window) select the **Edit**, **Copy** command. Then use the **Edit**, **Paste** command from the destination window menu bar. Any selected icons will be immediately copied.

**Using the keyboard** select the files to copy and press the <Ctrl+C> keyboard shortcut. Then select the destination window and press <Ctrl+V> to paste the files there.

**Using the mouse** is usually the easiest way of doing things. Dragging selected files from one window to another, with the left mouse button and the <Ctrl> key depressed, will copy them between windows, or folders, of the same drive.

Dragging can be a little confusing until you get used to Windows 95, because to drag-copy files to a folder or window of another disc drive, you don't have to hold down the <Ctrl> key. This, as we shall see, is the same action as drag-moving files between folders of the same drive. Until you get used to this, take special care, or you will end up moving files instead of copying them.

One easy way of telling what action a drag operation will

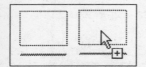 result in, is to look for a + sign on the drag pointer. This indicates that a copy is taking place. The example pointer on the left resulted from two files being copied between folders.

Perhaps a safer way of copying files with the mouse is to drag them with the right mouse button depressed. When you

have moved the pointer to the destination, releasing the mouse button produces the menu, shown here, which gives you a choice of operations. Moving the pointer to the **Copy Here** option and clicking, will complete the operation.

Practice all these methods and find which ones you are most confident with. Make sure that you actually copy several files into Practice folder, as we will need them later on.

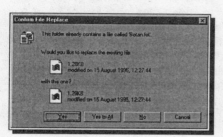

If you try to copy a file to a destination where a file with the same name already exists, you will be asked to confirm whether you want to overwrite the existing copy. The dialogue box shown here gives you several obvious choices. Selecting **Yes to All** will carry out replacement of any other files without asking for confirmation. A useful option, but use it with care. An overwritten file cannot be resurrected!

## Moving Files and Folders:

When you **copy** a file to somewhere else, the original version of the file is not altered or removed, but when you **move** a file to a new location, the original is actually deleted.

As with the copy operation there are many ways to move files about your system.

**Using the menu** of the source window select the **Edit**, **Cut** command. Then use the **Edit**, **Paste** command from the destination window menu bar.

**Using the keyboard** select the files to move and press the <Ctrl+X> keyboard shortcut. Then select the destination window and press <Ctrl+V> to paste the files there.

**Using the mouse** is usually the easiest way of doing things. Dragging selected files from one window to another, with the left mouse button depressed, will move them between windows, or folders, **of the same drive**. But don't forget that this same operation will **copy** files between different drives.

As with copying, dragging files with the right mouse button depressed but selecting the **Move Here** option from the menu produced, is maybe the safest way to carry out a file moving operation.

## Renaming Files and Folders:

You should by now have some files copied into your Practice folder and anything done to these files should not have any effect on the rest of your system.

Renaming a file is very easy. First click on the file icon to select it and then click the existing name below. This will place a rectangle around the name and put you into edit mode, as shown here. You then simply type in the new name and click somewhere else to finish the procedure. Another way is to select the file and use the **File**, **Rename** menu command. This puts you in the same edit mode, but just takes a little longer! Try them.

## Registering a File Type:

The file selected in the above example, Config.bak, is in fact a back-up copy we made of our Config.sys file, which is a system text file. (Do not bother looking for this file on your system). If we now decide that all our files with the extension '.bak' will be text files, it would be worthwhile to 'register' this file extension so that whenever we open such files, by double-clicking on their icons, they will be loaded into Notepad, the Windows text file editor.

To do this we would simply double-click the file icon to display the 'Open with' dialogue box shown on the facing page.

We would first type a **Description** in the top text box. This is the text that will show in future in the body of the list.

Next we would select NOTEPAD from the list, as shown. The easy way to do this is to move to the list and press the N key on the keyboard. As long as the **Always use this program to open this file** check box is ticked, clicking **OK** will then complete the registering process. Just to prove it has worked, Notepad will actually open and show the file contents, ready for editing.

If you carried out this operation, you would see that the file icon had changed to show the connection between this file type and the Notepad application, and the file name would also no longer show its extension.

To remove, or edit, this file type entry, use the **View**, **Options** menu command from any My Computer window and click the File Types tab, as described on page 40. Perhaps, if you have worked through this section, the entries on this dialogue box window will mean more to you, than they did then!

We could also have carried out this whole procedure by clicking the **New Type** button, but we would then have had to complete a fairly 'heavy' set of dialogue box text. The practical way seems much easier to us.

## File Properties:

If you want to know more about a particular file you have two ways of going about it.

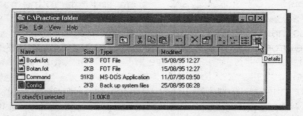

Using the **View**, **Details** menu command, or clicking the Details toolbar button, will display the files in a folder as shown above. Don't forget that you control whether the toolbar is displayed from the **View** menu. This listing shows a file's icon, name, size, type and when it was last modified.

To see even more information on a file, select it in the list, and click the Properties toolbar button, which opens the Properties box for the file, as shown below.

This lists the full properties of the file, including its full MS-DOS name, the dates when it was created, last modified and last accessed, and also allows you to change its attributes.

Also, if the file had been a DOS executable file (a program file that you can run) these properties would include several extra tabbed sheets giving you absolute control over how the program would run in an MS-DOS window. This is covered in more detail in a later chapter.

Before you close the properties sheet, move your mouse pointer over the Location line. A small yellow flag, showing the full file path displays briefly.

## Creating Shortcuts:

With Windows 95 you can put a shortcut to any program, document, or printer on your desktop or in any folder. shortcuts are quick ways to get to the items you use often. They save you having to dig deep into your system files to access them.

One program we seem to use a lot to process our system text files is the Notepad, so we will step through the process of placing a shortcut to it onto the desktop.

You must first find the actual program. An easy way is to open My Computer and look in the Windows folder of the C drive (or whichever drive Windows is installed on). With this folder open, press the N key until the Notepad icon is highlighted, or find it using the scroll bars.

Now, right-drag the Notepad icon (with the right mouse button depressed) onto the desktop, release the mouse button and click the **Create Shortcut(s) Here** menu option, as shown. This places the new shortcut icon on the desktop. Note that it has a right pointer arrow on it. This is how you can tell that an icon is a shortcut, not the original thing. If you find the icon name a little lengthy, you can rename it, using the same procedure as described earlier for renaming files.

If your desktop does not let you place its icons where you want to, you need to change its settings. Right-click on the desktop, click the **Arrange Icons** option on the command menu and click **Auto Arrange** to remove the tick mark alongside it, as shown here.

You should now be able to arrange your desktop icons in any way you wish, by simply dragging them around the desktop.

## Sending Files and Folders:

A very useful new feature of Windows 95 is the ability to quickly send files and folders to specific destinations. Right

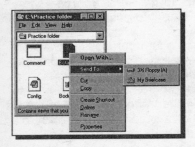

clicking a selected file, or files, will open the menu shown on the left. Selecting the **Send To** option opens the list of available destinations. At the moment, ours shows only two of these.

Selecting the **3½ Floppy (A)** option will copy any selected files and folders to a removable disc in the A drive, as shown by the very

decorative animated window that appears while the process is being carried out.

It is easy to add more locations to the Send To menu, as it is controlled by the contents of the

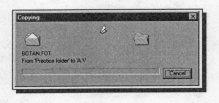

SendTo folder, which is itself in the Windows folder. You should by now, have no trouble finding and opening this folder using My Computer. Yours will probably only contain the same two shortcut icons as ours, shown here. You have

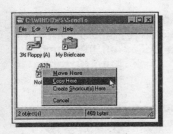

probably worked out by now, that every shortcut held in this folder produces an option on the Send To menu.

It is useful to be able to send text files straight to the Notepad so that you can see, and maybe edit, their contents. To add Notepad to the Send To menu, simply copy

the shortcut to Notepad icon from your desktop to the SendTo window. When you next open the menu it should have the extra item as shown here, on the right.

48

## Deleting Files and Folders:

Now we have finished with the files in the Practice folder we can remove, or delete, them. To do this, highlight the files you want to delete, and then either press the <Delete> key,

or use the **File**, **Delete** command from a window menu bar. Both methods open the message box shown here which gives you the chance to abort the operation by selecting **No**. To carry on with the deletion select **Yes**.

## The Recycle Bin:

Recycle Bin

As you can see from the above message box, by default all files deleted from a hard disc are actually placed in a holding folder named the Recycle Bin. Waste Basket would be a better name for this, but Macintosh computers use this and Apple won a court case about its use! That is probably why the Recycle Bin is the only Windows 95 desktop object that you cannot easily rename.

If you open the Recycle Bin, by double-clicking it, you will see that it is just a special folder. It lists all the files, folders, icons and shortcuts that have been deleted since it was last emptied, as shown below.

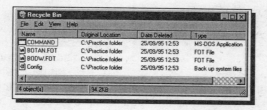

Note that it keeps a record of the original locations, so that it can restore them if necessary. To restore a file, select it, right click it and choose **Restore** from the menu.

You must **Empty Recycle Bin**, from its right-click menu, fairly often to save hard disc space.

## Formatting Discs

We assume, here, that your hard disc has already been formatted according to your manufacturer's instructions when setting up the system. New floppy discs must be formatted before they can be used by your computer's operating system. A floppy disc that has been formatted in one type of computer, can only be used in another computer if they are compatible and use the same operating system.

To format a floppy disc, put it into the correct disc drive, open My Computer by double-clicking its icon and right click on the icon for the drive. In our case, this would be the A drive, as shown above. From the command menu produced, select the **Format** option, which opens the dialogue box below. It only remains now to choose options in this box and press **Start** to carry out the formatting.

The **Capacity** drop down list lets you select the size of disc to format.

In the Format type section, the **Quick (erase)** option deletes the File Allocation Table of a previously formatted disc. You cannot use this on a new disc. **Full** carries out a full format, which will destroy any files on the disc (so take care). With a floppy disc this option then scans the disc for bad sectors. The **Copy system files only** option places the system files onto an already formatted disc, so that it can then be used as a start-up disc.

If you want to name your disc, so that the system will recognise it by that name (in the My Computer windows, for example), enter the name in the **Label** text box. Only 11

50

characters will be recognised here, as with older versions of MS-DOS. If not click the **No Label** option.

If you select **Display summary when finished** a result sheet, like the one shown here, will report on the format operation. Click the **Close** button to continue.

To make a system start-up disc from new, use the **Copy system files** option which places the required system files on the disc as well as formatting it.

If you prefer, of course, you can still use the Format command from an MS-DOS window. Chapter 10 lists all the switches that are then available.

## Copying Discs

Copying whole floppy discs is quite straightforward with Windows 95. It is best carried out from the menu opened when you right-click the disc drive icon, shown at the top of

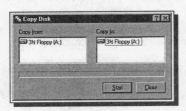

the previous page. Put the disc to copy into the drive and select **Copy Disk** from the menu.

A box, similar to that shown here, will open with your floppy disc drives listed. In our case, only one drive type shows on each side. If you have more, select the drive to **Copy from** and that to **Copy to**, but the drives must be of the same type. You can't carry out this operation between say 3.5" and 5.25" drives.

When ready, click the **Start** button. You will be told when to insert the destination disc, but be warned, any files already on the disc will be lost.

If you have upgraded to Windows 95 from a much older version of MS-DOS you will be happy with this process as it copies the whole disc at once. Unfortunately you do not have the option to make multiple copies from the original.

# Windows Explorer

Windows Explorer is the other way of manipulating your system data, you can see both the hierarchy of folders on your computer (and network) and all the files and folders in each selected folder. This can be confusing to start with, but it is especially useful for very quickly copying and moving files, as we shall see.

As with other system windows, the toolbar and the **View** menu, let you view your folder contents in four ways, large icons, small icons, list, and detailed list. The detailed view, however, provides extra information about your folder contents, such as:

Drive sizes and their free space, including mapped network drives, are listed in My Computer's contents.

Descriptions of the Control Panel tools are provided.

Jobs in the print queue are listed in the Printers folder.

Comments on other networked computers in the Network Neighbourhood can be viewed.

Folder contents can easily be sorted by name, size, type, and modification date, simply by clicking the column title.

Files retain their identifying icons.

All the powerful right-click and properties features described previously are supported in the Windows Explorer.

To open Windows Explorer from the desktop, click the START button, point to **Programs** and click Windows Explorer, which is probably very near the bottom of the program list.

You can also open the Explorer from within a My Computer desktop window, by selecting the folder to view and using the **File**, **Explore** menu option of the window.

When it starts, Windows Explorer shows a split window with the hierarchical 'system tree' appearing on the left, and the contents of drives and folders on the right. Your system will obviously display different contents from ours, shown on the next page, as it is bound to be structured differently.

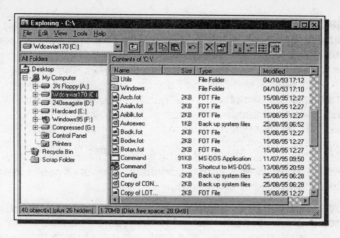

The system tree, in the left pane, lists all the resources of your computer, as well as those of a network you might be connected to. Objects which are marked with a plus sign (+), contain sub-folders. Clicking a (+) sign, opens it up to reveal the sub-folders beneath.

When sub-folders are displayed, the (+) sign changes to a minus sign (−), indicating that the parent folder can be collapsed. This is shown in the example on the left, where the drive F (containing the Windows 95 CD-ROM) is expanded.

The right-hand, or contents, pane is automatically displayed when you select a folder from the tree. As with most Windows 95 system windows, you can change the format of the information shown in the contents pane by using the **View** commands from the menu bar.

To get used to the Windows Explorer, we suggest you open it, maximise its window, set the contents format to **Details** from the **View** menu, and then slowly work your way down the system tree viewing in detail all your folders and files.

53

## Manipulating Files and Folders

To give an idea of the power of the Explorer we will step through a few file manipulation examples. To do this, first place an empty, but formatted, disc in your A floppy drive.

## Creating a Folder:

Click the A drive icon in the left pane of Windows Explorer to select it and then either:

issue the **File**, **New**, **Folder** menu command, or

right click in the empty contents pane and select **New**, **Folder** from the object menu.

Both methods place a folder, named New Folder, on the disc in the A drive. Rename this folder by typing 'Practice folder' in the highlighted name box and pressing the <Enter> key.

## Copying and Moving Files and Folders:

Now we must select some files and/or folders in the right pane that we want to copy to the floppy drive.

In the left pane, click the (+) sign alongside the C drive icon to open up one level of the tree. Open the Windows folder, in the same way, and click the Command folder to open its contents in the right pane. This folder actually contains all the MS-DOS command files, so make sure you don't delete any of the files, at this stage!

If you look at the status bar it will show how many files are in the folder (ours shows 36 plus 7 hidden) and how much space they take up on the disc (1.23 MB).

Now, move to the left pane in the Explorer and use the scroll bar and, if necessary, the (+) icons to make sure the destination folder, (in this case Practice folder on the A drive), is visible in the tree. At this stage, do **NOT** click any of the drive or folder names, or else you will have to start again.

Go back to the right pane and select several files in the list, as described earlier in the chapter (for contiguous ones, by clicking the first one and with the <Shift> key depressed, clicking the last; or for non-contiguous ones, by clicking them one at a time with the <Ctrl> key continuously depressed).

Now the panes are set up, so right-drag the selected files from the right pane to the left and when the Practice folder icon is highlighted, release the mouse button. This opens an option menu as shown below.

To copy the files you simply click the **Copy Here** option. If you had wanted to move them, you would obviously have chosen **Move Here**.

We think this is the easiest and, more important for a new user, the safest way of copying and moving files with the Windows Explorer, but you can also use any of the other methods described earlier in the chapter.

## Deleting Files and Folders:

Clicking the Practice folder icon in the left pane, should prove that the copied files did make it to their destination. You almost certainly do not want these MS-DOS files on your precious floppy disc, so we will delete them again.

Select one of them in the right Explorer pane and press the <Delete> key, or use the **File**, **Delete** menu command. In this case it is safe to accept **Yes** in the Confirm File Delete box, but take care with this warning in future.

Note that the file was deleted, not placed in the Recycle Bin. The Recycle Bin is not used when deletions are made from floppy discs. Another reason for taking extra care.

Now click the A drive icon in the left pane, select the folder shown in the contents section and delete it. Deleting a folder deletes all its contents as well. But you are given lots of warnings.

## Using Quick View

You may have noticed that some menus produced by right-clicking on a file have an option to **Quick View** the file. This means that Windows 95 can look into that file type and show you its contents, without actually opening it. The program comes with about 20 drivers to give access to different file types, as listed in Appendix B. If you are lucky your favourite application program will be one of them. If not, be patient, as many more are expected to be added to the list.

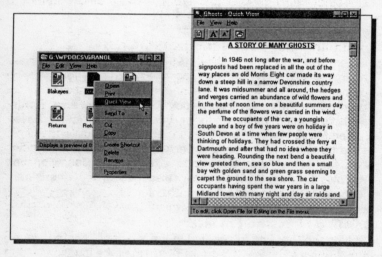

The composite above shows a Quick View of a WordPerfect 6.0 document and the desktop window it was opened from.

You can also Quick View into executable files (with the extensions .COM and .EXE) with this facility. This can sometimes be useful to see the file header information.

# 4. CONTROLLING WINDOWS OPERATION

## Printing with Windows 95

The printing operation with Windows 95 is vastly improved over previous versions of both Windows and DOS. Its new 32-bit printing architecture supports pre-emptive multitasking which provides improved printing performance, much smoother printing in the background, and a quicker return to your work after a print job is started.

## Installing and Configuring a Printer

When you installed Windows 95 your printers should have been installed as well. If you upgraded from an earlier version of Windows, this would have happened automatically. If not you would have been stepped through the Add Printer Wizard, described later.

Over 800 different printers are supported by Windows 95 so, hopefully, you shouldn't have too much trouble getting

yours to work. The printer and printing functions are now included in a single Printers folder, which you can open by double-clicking the above icon in the My Computer window. Our Printers folder, shown on the right, has four printers available for use, and an Add Printer icon. This folder provides an easy way of adding new printers, configuring existing ones, and managing all your print jobs.

Windows 95 supports the following printer set-up methods:

• Plug and Play printers are automatically detected at installation time, or during the boot up process. You will be prompted for the necessary driver files if they are not already in the Windows directory, these should be supplied with a new Plug-and Play printer.

- Point and Print printing enables you to quickly connect to, and use, printers shared on some other networked PCs. When you connect to a shared printer, Windows automatically copies and installs the correct driver for the shared printer. You can then simply begin printing.

- For other situations, the Add Printer Wizard steps you through the printer installation process, whether the new printer is connected to your PC, or on a network.

To 'manually' install a new printer to your set up, double-click the **Add Printer** icon in the Printers window. This opens the Wizard shown here, which really makes the installation procedure much easier than it used to be. As with all Wizards you progress from screen to screen by clicking the **Next** button. The first time you do this, you have to wait a short time, while the printer driver information database is built.

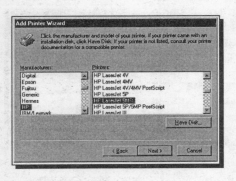

The next dialogue box lets you choose the make and model of printer you want to install. In our case we are setting up a Hewlett Packard (HP in the list) model LaserJet 5MP. If you have a disc of drivers that came with the printer, put it in the floppy drive and click the **Have Disk** button.

You are next asked to select the correct Port. This refers to the socket at the back of your PC which is connected to the printer. For a stand alone set-up this would usually be the

LPT1 port. (Short for Line Printer No.1). Next you can customise the printer name, maybe on a network, it would be useful to describe where it is actually located.

You should then accept **Yes** to have a test print carried out, to check that all is OK with the installation. When you click the **Finish** button a new icon will be placed in your Printers folder and, as long as the printer is switched on, a test page should be produced.

Hopefully, this test should give an impressive demonstration of the printer's capabilities and you will be able to answer **Yes** when asked if the test was successful. If not, click the **No** button, and Windows 95 will attempt to sort out the problem for you.

**Configuring your Printer** - All configuration for a printer is now consolidated onto a tabbed property sheet that is accessed from its icon in the Printers folder. Right clicking a printer icon opens the object menu, shown on the left, which gives control of the printers operation. If you click the **Properties** option, the sheet

shown on the right opens and lets you control all the printer's parameters, such as the printer port (or network path), paper and graphics options, built in fonts, and other device options specific to the printer model. All these settings are fairly self explanatory and as they depend on your printer type we will let you work them out for yourselves.

If you use one printer all, or most of the time, you should make it the default printer, by selecting **Set as De_f_ault** from its object (or right-click) menu. This saves continually having to select that printer from within your applications.

Once you have installed and configured your printers in Windows they are then available for all your application programs to use. For new users upgrading from DOS, this will be an enormous improvement. Gone are the days you will need to battle to get printing every time you install a new program. If Windows is happy with your printer set-up, all its applications should be as well. Just make sure that the correct printer is selected by the program, which is usually one of the program's **F_ile** menu options.

## Managing Print Jobs:

Selecting **O_pen** from a printer's right-click object menu, or double-clicking the printer icon, will open its window.

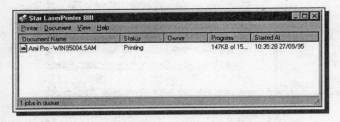

As shown above, this displays detailed information about the contents of any work actually being printed, or of print jobs that are waiting in the queue. This includes the name of the document, its status and 'owner', when it was added to the print queue, the number of pages and size of the document, and the priority of the print job.

You can control the printing operation from the **P_rinter** and **Document** menu options of this window, or from the right-click object menu of a particular printer's icon. Selecting **P_ause Printing** will stop the operation until you make the same selection again. It is a toggle menu option. The **P_urge Print Jobs** option will remove all, or selected, print jobs from the print queue.

## The Control Panel

Control Panel

The Windows 95 Control Panel is a special folder that provides a quick and easy way to change the hardware and software settings of your system.

To access the Control Panel, double-click its icon, shown here, which you will find in the My Computer window. This opens a window, similar to the following. The actual options available will depend on your particular system set-up, so they may not be quite the same. The two windows below show the Control Panel with different **View** settings. The upper with **Large Icons** and the other in **Details** view, which describes each panel option.

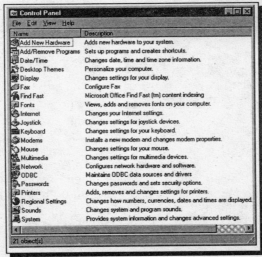

Double-clicking any of the Control Panel icons allows you (in order of icon appearance on our PC) to:

add new hardware, set up software programs, change the date and time of your system, change the appearance of your display, control a fax, view and change system fonts, change Internet settings, control your joystick, keyboard, modem and mouse settings, change settings for multi-media devices, configure network settings, maintain ODBC data sources, maintain system passwords, install and configure your printer(s), specify international settings, such as the formatting of numbers and dates, specify Windows sounds for different actions and maintain general system information.

## Checking your Regional Settings

Most Windows application programs use Windows settings to

determine how they display and handle, time, date, language, numbers, and currency.

It is important that you ensure your system was correctly set-up during the installation process.

From the Control Panel, double-click the Regional Settings icon, to open the Properties sheet shown here.

Make sure your country setting is correct, if not, change it by clicking the down arrow to the right of the drop-down list and select the most appropriate country. You will have to restart Windows before any changes become effective.

Before leaving the Properties sheet, work your way through the tabbed pages and make sure the selections are as you want them. If, in the future, you start getting '$' signs, instead of '£' signs, or commas in numbers where you would expect periods, check your regional settings.

## Adding Hardware to your System

If you can afford the luxury of a complete multi-media PC with all the trimmings when you first buy your computer you may never need to add any more hardware. But, if not, have you ever tried to add a sound card or a modem to your system? If so, it was almost certainly a nightmare to get everything working again, unless you were very lucky.

All hardware has to communicate with the processor of your PC, to send and receive messages and data. This communication is done by a series of interrupts or memory accesses. All the hardware components must be configured correctly or they will interfere with each other. Not many PC users understand, or even want to know about, this.

Windows 95 has gone some way to overcome these problems and make it much easier to add to your system without having to tear your hair out as well.

### Plug-and-Play:

Windows 95 is the first PC operating system to include a set of standards for software controlling the settings of suitably designed hardware devices. When you add a Plug-and-Play compatible device to your system, Windows takes charge and automatically controls all its settings so that it fits in with the rest of the system. So, when you buy new hardware, make sure that it is Plug-and-Play compatible. Microsoft are planning to add this facility to Windows NT in the near future, so the standard will very rapidly be accepted by all the main manufacturers.

### Add New Hardware Wizard:

Add New
Hardware

If you are not lucky and your new hardware is not Plug-and-Play compatible all is not lost, as there is now a very powerful Wizard to step you through the process of installing new hardware.

If at all possible, fit the new tackle before you run the Wizard. It is just possible that Windows will recognise the change and be able to carry out the configuration itself.

To start the Wizard, double-click the Add New Hardware icon in the Control Panel, read the text and click **Next** to open the following screen. Make sure you have no applications running, and as long as you have actually installed the new

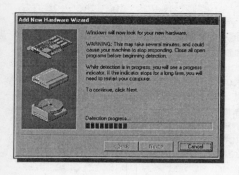

hardware select **Yes** to have the Wizard search your system for anything new.

The search procedure can take several minutes to complete. A progress bar, shown here, lets you know how things are going. The hard disc will also make enough noise to keep you awake! Eventually you should be given a list of any new hardware additions that are recognised. Select what you want to install and click the **Next** button.

If the search procedure goes very dead on you, you will have to re-start your PC and try the manual option. Hopefully this will not be necessary.

## Adding Software

Add/Remove
Programs

Installing Windows applications is now very easy with Windows 95. Place the first disc or the CD-ROM with the software on it in its drive, double-click the Add/ Remove Programs icon in the Control Panel and select **Install** from the Install/Uninstall tabbed sheet, shown here. The disc drives will be searched and you will be asked to confirm what you want installed.

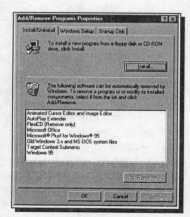

The Uninstall option only works for programs on your system that were specially written for Windows 95.

These are listed at the bottom of the dialogue box. This uninstall procedure removes all trace of the selected program from your hard disc. With programs written for Windows 95, you will not get left with hundreds of application set-up files on your system, that you don't know what to do with. Non Windows 95 programs will still give this problem though.

## Adding/Removing Windows Features

The Windows Setup tab of the Add/Remove Programs sheet allows you to install, or remove, Windows components at any time. If you do not have a described feature on your system it may not have been installed. Open the sheet, shown below on the right, highlight the group that you think will contain it

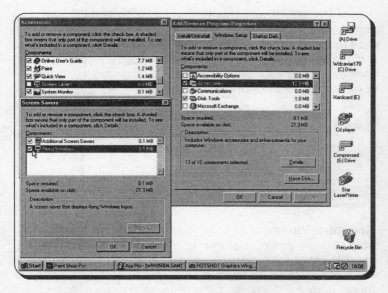

and click the **Details** button. This will list the components of the chosen group. Click the box to the left of an item name. Newly ticked items will be installed, and any with their ticks removed, will be un-installed.

It is easy to use up too much hard disc space with Windows 95 features, so keep your eye on the **Space required** section. You will need to have the CD-ROM or

65

original system discs available, and when you have made the selections you want, keep clicking **OK** to carry out your changes.

## Customising the Desktop
We could write a separate book on this subject, and maybe we will in the future, but at this stage we will just touch on some of the options available. The screen shot below shows the simple desktop we use most of the time.

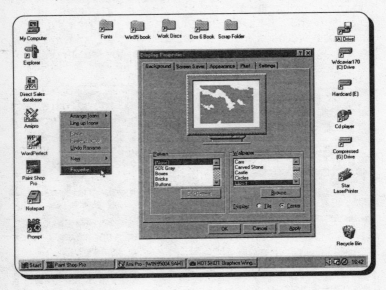

## Shortcut Icons:
This shows a range of shortcuts to the main system facilities, spaced around the edge, leaving space in the middle for the application window we are using. Other open applications are reduced to the Taskbar. One click on them will open them instantly.

If you can't remember how to create shortcuts, look back at page 47. Our desktop above is in danger of being swamped with them, maybe we will soon have to put all the folders at the moment along the top, in their own folder. They will then be easily available, but take up much less room.

## Changing the Background:

Right-clicking on the desktop and selecting **Properties** from the object menu, opens the tabbed Display Properties sheets, as shown on the facing page. This gives you the option of choosing or editing a desktop **Pattern**, but we always set this option to (None). Browsing through the **Wallpaper** list shows some interesting displays in the sample at the top of the box. The Clouds option is new with Windows 95 and is actually part of the opening screen. If you select this it goes quite well with our layout of shortcut icons.

The ScreenSaver tab lets you select from several savers provided with Windows. These are graphics which are loaded to the screen when it has been inactive for a while.

The Appearance tab, shown here, lets you choose from a range of rather garish colour options in the **Scheme** list box.

You can select window components in the **Item** list and change their **Color**, and sometimes their **Size** and **Font**.

The colour of our desktop is set to white as shown in this example. The other window components are left with their default settings.

The Settings tab gives you some control over the screen resolution used with the **Desktop Area** slider. This will show the available options open to you, depending on your monitor type, your graphics card and the **Color Palette** setting you have chosen. Unless you have a very powerful graphics card with a lot of built-in memory, the more colours you use the less the screen resolution will be. Our example shows 256 colours at a resolution of 800 by 600 pixels. Our system is

67

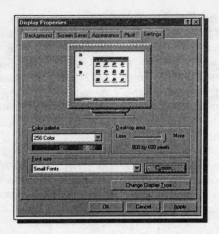

quite happy with a resolution of 1024 by 768 pixels and 16-bit colour, but the screen dumps for this book would be unreadable.

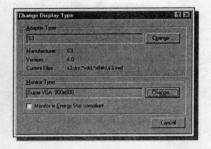

One thing to check on this sheet is that your monitor type is selected correctly.

Clicking the **Change Display Type** button will open the dialogue box shown here above. This shows an S3 **Adapter Type** is fitted. Click the

**Change** button alongside the **Monitor Type** box. You may

find that your monitor type is listed and that you get a better performance by using it. If your type is not listed select one of the standard ones listed on the right. They seem to work well for us!

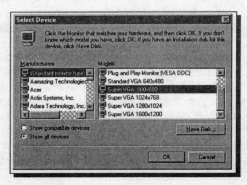

## Changing the Taskbar Menus

The Taskbar menu system, as we saw in an earlier chapter, is set up originally when Windows 95 is installed. The START menu being standard, but the **Programs** cascade menus being based on any previous Windows set-up you had on your computer. Once you are a little familiar with the new Windows, we are sure you will want to tailor these menus to your own preferences.

## Adding to the START Menu:

It is very easy to add extra programs to the top of the START menu. This can be useful, as this menu opens with one click of the START button which gives very rapid access to its contents.

To do this, you can simply drag the program icon, or a shortcut to it, onto the START button itself. For example, to add the Windows text editor WordPad to the START menu, open the C:\Program Files\Accessories folder with My

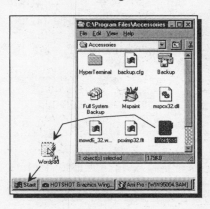

Computer as shown here. This is the Accessories folder, in the Program Files folder which is on the C drive.

Find the WordPad icon and drag it with the left mouse button depressed. When you drag a single icon like this, the drag pointer changes as you move round the screen, to indicate what will happen if you release the mouse button at that location. As shown above, the pointer is over the desktop and the small black arrow '↗' in its bottom right corner shows that a shortcut would be produced. Over some desktop features the arrow changes to a plus sign '+' showing that the file would be copied there. Drag the icon slowly over the START button. It will first seem to go under the button, then it will change to a 'No entry' sign '⊘' when

over the Taskbar border, but will finally show the shortcut arrow. At that point, release the mouse button. Your START menu should now have an extra option at the top, as shown here.

Within reason, you can add as many extra items to the START menu as you like and they will sort themselves in alphabetical order.

The Taskbar Properties sheet lets you both add and remove items to and from the START and the **Programs** menu. To open this sheet, you select **Properties** from the Taskbar right-click menu.

Clicking the **Add** button steps you, in a 'Wizard like' way, through the process of creating a shortcut to the program you want, and adding it to the required menu position. The **Remove** button lets you choose a menu item and then deletes it from the menu system.

The **Advanced** button can be used to manipulate the menus in an Explorer window, as shown below. If you are happy using the Windows Explorer, this is by far the quickest way to customise your menus. This method is possible because these menus depend on the contents of the Start Menu sub-folder of the Windows folder. Menu items are stored here as shortcuts and you can add or delete them as you want.

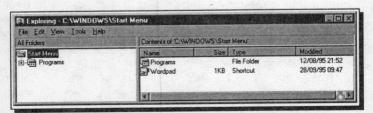

# 5. WINDOWS 95 ACCESSORIES

Windows 95 includes a set of redesigned applications and utilities that come in 32-bit code and support multitasking, long filenames, OLE 2, and other Win32 features.

Although very useful, these 'applets' will not fully satisfy the needs of advanced users. But no doubt Microsoft, and other third-party developers, will be flooding the market with new Windows 95 applications and utilities that do.

## WordPad

Wordpad

A new text editor, WordPad, replaces the Write accessory of earlier Windows versions. This is not a fully featured word processor, as it has no pagination features, but is useful for creating simple documents and memos. It is also easily integrated with Microsoft Exchange to allow users to send e-mail, or fax files directly from the editor.

WordPad allows you to enhance text, to use different size fonts within the same document, and using OLE (Object Linking and Embedding), to link and embed objects such as graphics, created in other Windows applications.

As it uses the new common dialogue boxes for opening, saving, and printing files, long filenames, and is an OLE server and client application, we will use WordPad to demonstrate the use of some of these features in Windows 95. Also, getting used to one Windows application is a good introduction to most others, as there are many common features shared by them all.

WordPad 'fully' supports four file formats, in that it will both read them from and write them to disc.

Text files, both ANSI and ASCII formats

Microsoft Word for Windows version 6 files

Rich text format files (RTF), a format which most other word processors can handle.

It will also read files created in Microsoft Write (.WRI), but unfortunately, cannot save in that format.

# WordPad Basics

To access the text editor click WordPad in the Accessories Program group of the START menu. An application window similar to that shown below will appear, and an un-named document will open on your screen. When you save your work later you should give this document a meaningful name so that you can identify its contents.

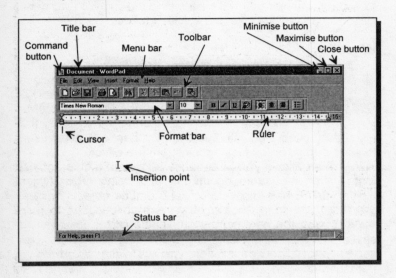

## The WordPad Screen:

The top line of the WordPad screen is the Title bar which contains the name of the document. If this bar is dragged with the mouse, the window can be moved around the screen. Also, just like any other window, its size can be changed by dragging any of its four sides, or the sizing tab, in the required direction.

The next line down is the Menu bar which allows access to the following sub menus:

File Edit View Insert Format Help

As described in Chapter 2 - 'Working with Windows 95' - the sub-menus are accessed either with your mouse, or by pressing the <Alt> key followed by the underlined letter.

## The Toolbar:

As with most Windows 95 windows, the Toolbar contains a set of icon buttons that you click to carry out some of the more common menu functions. The actions of each icon are outlined in the following illustration.

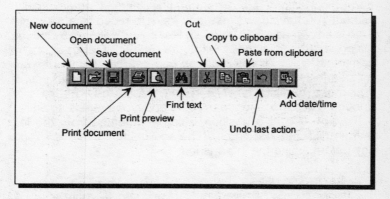

## The Format Bar:

WordPad has an extra bar of icons that are used to more easily control the format of text in a document.

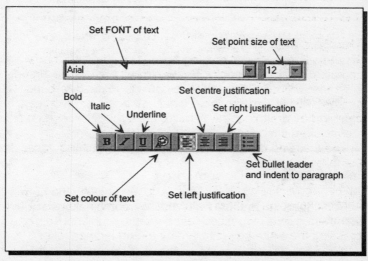

## Entering Text:

Before going any further, type the memo displayed below. The text may not be very relevant to you, but will be used to illustrate some of WordPad's capabilities.

As you type in text, any time you want to force a new line, or paragraph, just press <Enter>. While typing within a paragraph, WordPad sorts out line lengths automatically, without you having to press any keys to move to a new line. This is known as 'word wrap'. In fact if you look in the Options dialogue box, opened with the **View**, **Options** menu command, you will see that you can set different word wrap options for each of the file formats that WordPad can use. If you make a mistake while typing, press the <BkSp> key enough times to erase the mistake and type the text again.

To type text at a position which is indented from the left margin (like the last entry of the text below), use the <Tab> key before typing the information.

---

MEMO TO PC USERS
The microcomputers in the Data Processing room are a mixture of IBM compatible PCs with either 486 or Pentium processors. They all have 3.5" floppy drives (of 1.44MB capacity), some also have CD-ROM drives, and others have 5.25" high density drives (of 1.2MB capacity). The PCs are connected to various printers, the Laser printers available give the best results, but are more expensive to use.

The computer you are using will have at least a 500MB hard disc on which a number of software programs, including a version of Windows, have been installed. To make life easier, the hard disc is highly structured with each program installed in a separate directory. When first switched on, the following prompt is displayed:

C:\>

---

## Moving Around a Document:

You can move the cursor around a document with the normal direction keys, as well as with the key combinations shown opposite.

74

| To move | Press |
|---------|-------|
| Left one character | ← |
| Right one character | → |
| Up one line | ↑ |
| Down one line | ↓ |
| Left one word | Ctrl+← |
| Right one word | Ctrl+→ |
| To beginning of line | Home |
| To end of line | End |
| To previous paragraph | Ctrl+↑ |
| To next paragraph | Ctrl+↓ |
| Up one window | Page Up |
| Down one window | Page Down |
| To top of window | Ctrl+Page Up |
| To bottom of window | Ctrl+Page Down |
| To beginning of file | Ctrl+Home |
| To end of file | Ctrl+End |

## Saving to a File:

To save a document, use the **File, Save** command, or click the Save toolbar icon. A dialogue box appears on the screen, as shown below, with the cursor in the **File name** field box waiting for you to type a name. You can select a folder, or drive, other than the one displayed, in the usual Windows 95 way as used in all My Computer windows.

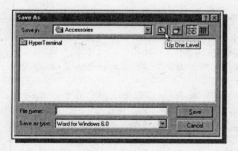

To save your work, move the cursor into the **File name** box, and type **PC Users example 1**. This is an example of a long filename, which can be up to 255 characters in length. You should remember, however, that long filenames in Windows 95 are now case sensitive.

75

There are four formatting choices in the **Save as type** box when you first save a WordPad document:

| *Use* | *To Save As* |
|---|---|
| Word for Windows 6 | To save your file in the format used by Word for Windows 6. It can then be used in that program |
| Rich Text Format (RTF) | A Rich Text Format file that retains most of its text enhancements and can be imported into many applications |
| Text document | A Windows ANSI file. Use this option if your document is a program or you intend to tele-communicate it. |
| Text - MS-DOS format | An unformatted ASCII file. |

To save your document in the future with a different name use the **File**, **Save As** menu command.

## Document Editing

For small deletions, such as letters or words, the easiest way is to use the <Delete> or <BkSp> keys. With the <Delete> key, position the cursor on the first letter you want to remove and press <Delete>; the letter is deleted and the following text moves one space to the left. With the <BkSp> key, position the cursor immediately to the right of the character to be deleted and press <BkSp>; the cursor moves one space to the left pulling the rest of the line with it and overwriting the character to be deleted. Note that the difference between the two is that with <Delete> the cursor does not move at all.

Text editing is usually carried out in the insert mode. Any characters typed will be inserted at the cursor location and the following text will be pushed to the right, and down.

Pressing the <Insert> key will change to Overstrike mode, entered text then overwrites any existing text at the cursor.

When larger scale editing is needed, use the **Cut, Copy** and **Paste** operations, the text to be altered must be 'selected' before the operation can be carried out. These functions are then available when the **Edit** sub-menu is activated, or Toolbar icons are used.

## Selecting Text:

The procedure in WordPad, as in all Windows applications, is that before any operation such as formatting or editing can be carried out on text, you first select the text to be altered. Selected text is highlighted on the screen. This can be carried out in several ways:

    a.   **Using the keyboard**; position the cursor on the first character to be selected, hold down the <Shift> key while using the direction keys to highlight the required text, then release the <Shift> key. Navigational key combinations can also be used with the <Shift> key to highlight blocks of text.

    b.   **With the mouse**; click the left mouse button at the beginning of the block and drag the cursor across the block so that the desired text is highlighted, then release the mouse button. To select a word, double-click in the word, to select a larger block, place the cursor at the beginning of the block, and with the <Shift> key depressed, move the mouse pointer to the end of the desired block, and click the left mouse button.

        **Using the 'selection area' and a mouse**; place the mouse pointer in the left margin area of the WordPad window where it changes to a right slanting arrow, and click the left mouse button once to select the current line, twice to select the current paragraph, or three times to select the whole document.

Try out all these methods and find out the one you are most comfortable with.

## Copying Blocks of Text:

Once text has been selected it can be copied to another location in your present document, to another WordPad document, to another Windows application, or even to the desktop! As with most of the editing and formatting operations there are many ways of doing this.

The first is by using the **Edit, Copy** command sequence from the menu, or clicking the Copy Toolbar icon, moving the cursor to the start of where you want the copied text, and using the **Edit, Paste** command, or clicking the Paste icon.

Another method uses the quick key combinations, <Ctrl+C> to copy and <Ctrl+V> to paste.

To copy the same text again to another location in the document, move the cursor to the new location and paste it there with either of the above methods.

**Drag and Drop** - Maybe the easiest way to copy selected text, or an object such as a graphic, is to drag it with the left mouse button and the <Ctrl> key both depressed and to release the mouse button when the vertical line that follows the pointer is at the required destination.

As you get used to Windows 95 application packages you will be able to decide which of these methods is best for you.

### Moving Blocks of Text:

Selected text can also be moved, in which case it is deleted in its original location. Use the **Edit, Cut,** command, or the <Ctrl+X> keyboard shortcut, or click the Cut icon, move the cursor to the required new location and then use the **Edit, Paste** command, <Ctrl+V>, or click the Paste icon. The moved text will be placed at the cursor location and will force any existing text to make room for it. This operation can be cancelled by simply pressing <Esc>.

**Drag and Drop** - Selected text, or an object such as a graphic, can be moved by dragging it with the left mouse button depressed and releasing the button when the vertical line that follows the mouse pointer is at the required destination.

### Deleting Blocks of Text:

When text is deleted it is removed from the document. With WordPad any selected text can be deleted by pressing **Edit, Cut,** or by simply pressing the <Delete> key. However, using **Edit, Cut**, places the text on the Windows clipboard and allows you to use the **Edit, Paste** command, while using the <Delete> key, does not.

## The Undo Command:

As text is lost with the delete command you should use it with caution, but if you do make a mistake all is not lost as long as you act immediately. The **Edit, Undo** command, or Toolbar button, reverses your most recent action, so you need to use it before carrying out any further operations. The quick key for this command is <Ctrl+Z>.

## Finding and Changing Text:

WordPad allows you to search for specifically selected text, or character combinations. In the 'Find' mode it will highlight each occurrence in turn so that you can carry out some action on it. In the 'Replace' mode you specify what replacement is to be automatically carried out.

For example, in a long memo you may decide to replace every occurrence of the word 'programme' with the word 'program'. This is very easy to do. First go to the beginning of the document, as searches operate in a forward direction, then choose the **Edit**, **Replace** command from WordPad's

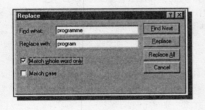

menu bar to open a dialogue box, like the one shown here.

You type what you want to search for in the **Find what** box. You can then specify whether you want to **Match whole word only**, and whether to **Match case**, (upper or lower case) by check-marking the appropriate boxes. Type the replacement word in the **Replace with** box, and then make a selection from one of the four buttons provided. Selecting **Replace** requires you to manually confirm each replacement, whilst selecting **Replace All** will replace all occurrences of the word automatically.

## Formatting Your Work

When working with text files you cannot format your documents, but in Word for Windows, or RTF modes, you can. Such formatting can involve the appearance of individual characters or words, and the indentation, addition of bullet leaders and the alignment of paragraphs. These functions are carried out in WordPad from the **Fo̱rmat** menu options or from the Format bar.

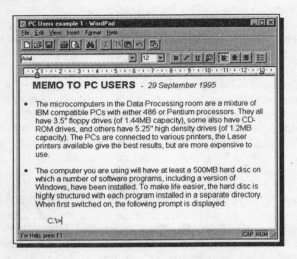

As an example of some of the formatting options, we have carried out some changes to the memo created earlier.

The title was highlighted, its point size changed to 16 and emboldened, by clicking format bar options. The date was then added to it by clicking the Date/Time icon on the Toolbar and choosing the date format required.

The two main paragraphs were then selected and the Bullet icon clicked on the Format bar. This indented the paragraphs and gave them bullet leaders, as shown.

Try these features out for yourself. They are quite powerful.

### The Ruler:

The Ruler, at the top of the text area of the WordPad window, lets you set and see Tab points for your text, or to visually change the left and right margins, (the empty space to the left and right of the text area) of your document.

Setting your own tabs is easy by clicking within the ruler where you want to set the tab. Tabs can be moved within the ruler by dragging them with the mouse to a new position, or removed by simply dragging them off the ruler. Default tab settings do not show on the ruler, but custom tabs do.

## Printing Documents

As long as your printer has been properly installed and configured, as described in the first few pages of Chapter 4, you should have no problems printing your document from the WordPad application.

### Setting up your Page:

Before attempting to print, make sure that WordPad is set to the same page size as the paper you plan to use.

To do this, open the following dialogue box with the **File**, **Page Setup** menu command.

In this box you can control your paper **Size** and **Source**, the size of all your **Margins** around the edge of your sheet, and the **Orientation** of the paper. **Portrait** has the longest dimension in a vertical direction, and **Landscape** has it in the horizontal. The example 'page' at the top of the box will show the effects of any changes. The **Printer** button lets you select between different printers, and set their properties.

### Print Preview:

Before actually committing yourself and printing your document to paper, it is always best to look at a Preview on the screen. This can save both your paper and printer toner or ribbon bills.

To preview the current document and settings, either click the Print Preview icon on the Toolbar, or use the **File**, **Print Preview** menu command.

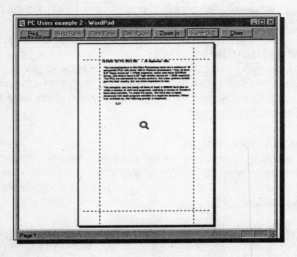

The preview screen, shown above, is the only place in WordPad that you can actually see your document's pagination, and then you have no control over it! A dreadful omission, but perhaps intentional, to make sure everyone buys Word for Windows instead!

To zoom in on the document, just click the pointer on it, or use the **Zoom In** button. If your document has several pages

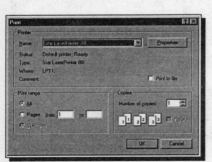

you can select a **Two Page** view of it. When you are happy your document is perfect, select **Print**, or if it needs more editing press the **Close** button.

In the final dialogue box, you select what to print and the number of copies. Select **Print to file** if you want to send print output to a file, and finally press **OK** to print it.

## The Windows Paint Program

Mspaint

Paint is a new 32-bit Windows 95 application, which replaces the previous Paintbrush. You can use Paint to create, view and edit, simple or complicated graphics.

Paint is an OLE (Object Linking and Embedding) server, and allows the creation of OLE object information that can be embedded or linked into other documents, as we shall see at the end of the chapter. Paint can read both PCX and BMP file formats, but can only write in the BMP format.

## Starting Paint:

To start Paint, open the START menu, select **Programs**, Accessories and then click the Paint entry. A few seconds later, the 'untitled - Paint' opening window will be displayed, as shown below.

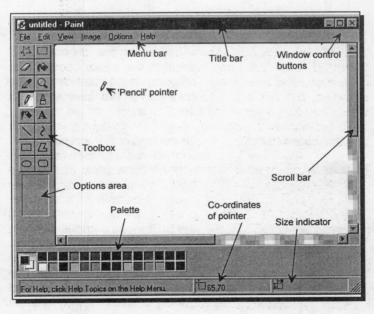

The window is divided into a 'drawing' area (the default size of which depends on your video display), surrounded by the

Menu bar at the top, the Palette at the bottom, the Options box at the bottom-left corner, with the Toolbox above it.

## The Paint Toolbox:

The drawing area is where you create your drawings with the help of various tools from the Toolbox. Note that the pencil tool is always selected when you start Paint, and that the function of a Toolbox icon is flagged when you move the mouse pointer over it.

To select a tool, simply point to it and click. Several of them have extra functions you can also select in the Options area. Some tools can work with either of the current foreground or background colours - dragging the tool with the left mouse button uses the foreground colour and with the right one the background colour.

More detail of the Toolbox functions is listed below.

| *Tool* | *Function* |
|---|---|
| Free Form select  | Used to cut-out an irregular-shaped area of a picture, with either an opaque or transparent background, which can then be dragged to another part of the drawing, or manipulated using the **Edit** menu commands. |
| Rectangle select  | Used to cut out a rectangular-shaped area of a picture, with either an opaque or transparent background, which can then be dragged to another part of the drawing, or manipulated using the **Edit** menu commands. |
| Eraser  | Used to change the selected foreground colours under the eraser icon to a background colour, or automatically change every occurrence of one colour in the drawing area to another. |

**Colour fill**

Used to fill in any closed shape or area with the current foreground or background colour.

**Pick colour**

Used to set the foreground or background colour to that at the pointer.

**Magnifier**

Used to zoom the image to different magnifications. Choose from 1x, 2x, 6x or 8x magnification in the options area.

**Pencil**

Used to draw free hand lines in either the foreground or background colour.

**Brush**

Used to draw free hand lines with a selection of tools and thicknesses shown in the options area.

**Airbrush**

Used to produce one of three available circular sprays in the foreground or background colours.

**Text**

Used to add text of different fonts, sizes and attributes in the current foreground colour, with either an opaque or transparent background.

**Line**

Used to generate straight lines between two points in the current foreground or background colours and drawing width.

**Curve**

Used to generate curved lines in the current colours and drawing width.

85

**Rectangle**

Used to draw hollow and filled rectangles or squares (<Shift> key depressed), in the current foreground or background colours and drawing width.

**Polygon**

Used to draw hollow and filled triangles and other polygon shapes, in the current foreground or background colours and drawing width.

**Ellipse**

Used to draw hollow and filled ellipses or circles (<Shift> key depressed), in the current foreground or background colours and drawing width.

**Rounded Rectangle**

Used to draw hollow and filled rectangles or squares (<Shift> key depressed), with rounded corners, in the current foreground or background colours and drawing width.

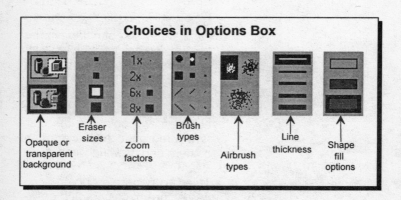

**Choices in Options Box**

Opaque or transparent background

Eraser sizes

Zoom factors

Brush types

Airbrush types

Line thickness

Shape fill options

## Preparing for a Drawing

Before you start drawing you may need to set the size of the image you want. To do this, use the **I**mage, **A**ttributes menu

command to open the dialogue box shown here.

The default **Width** and **Height** settings for a new image are given in pixels (**Pels**) and are the same as your screen resolution setting. If you need a specific image size when it is printed to paper you can work in **Inches** or **Cm**. Lastly in this box, you can set whether to work in colour on in black and white.

Clicking the **Default** button will make your new settings the default for any new working sessions.

## Selecting Working Colours:

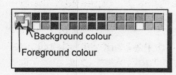

Background colour
Foreground colour

The current background and foreground colour settings are always shown in the two squares to the left of the palette, as shown here.

To select a new background colour, point to the colour in the Palette and click the right mouse button. If you now select the **F**ile, **N**ew command, Paint will open a new document with the selected background colour. Alternatively you could 'flood' the existing background by selecting the Colour fill icon and right-clicking it on the background of the drawing area

To select a different foreground colour to be used with any of the drawing tools in the Toolbox, point to the colour in the Palette and click the left mouse button.

## Entering Text in a Drawing:

If you intend to enter text within a drawing, carry out the following steps:

- Select the foreground colour for the text.

- Select the **Text** tool from the Toolbox.
- Select opaque or transparent from the options box.
- Click the pointer on the working area to open the text box, drag it to the correct size and type the text.
- Open the text toolbar with the **View**, **Text toolbar** menu command.
- Select the font, point size or other style you want to use from the text toolbar, as shown below.
- When you are happy with the text, click outside the text box to 'fix' it in the drawing and close the toolbar.

While the text toolbar is open you can change any of its options, or use the palette, and see the entered text change straight away.

In the future, as long as the **Text toolbar** option is ticked in the **View** menu, the toolbar will open whenever you start to enter text.

## Using the Paint Tools

Most of the other tools in Paint's Toolbox are quite easy and straightforward to use. To select a tool, point to it and click the left mouse button which depresses its icon in the Toolbox. To use them, you move the pointer to a suitable position within the drawing area and drag the tool around to accomplish the required task. With most of the options, dragging with the left mouse button uses the active foreground colour, and with the right button the active background colour. Releasing the mouse button stops the action being performed.

If you make a mistake, you can select the **Edit, Undo** command from the menu bar up to three times, to cancel the last three actions you carried out.

To complete this discussion, we need to describe how to use the 'Curve', and 'Polygon' tools, which differ slightly from the rest. For example:

**To draw a curve**, first click the Curve toolbar icon, choose a line thickness in the options box, click the pointer in the required starting position within the drawing area, then press the left mouse button to anchor the beginning of the curve and move the mouse to the required end of the eventual curve and release it. A 'flexible' line in the current foreground colour will be produced between the two points. Using the right mouse button will produce a line with the current background colour. Next, click one of the mouse buttons away from the line and drag it around the window, which causes the line to curve as you move the pointer. When you are happy with the produced curvature, release the mouse button.

**To draw a polygon**, place the Polygon pointer in the required starting point in the drawing area, press the mouse button for the foreground or background colour you want, drag the mouse to the required end of the first side of the polygon and release it. A line is produced between the two points. Next, continue adding sides to the polygon in this way until you complete it, at which point you should double-click the mouse button.

The best way of learning how to use the various drawing tools is to experiment. Try drawing something and practise with all the tools, before going on.

There is 'no limit' to what you can do with Paint. All you need is imagination, a lot of patience and some artistic ability! Having got you started, we will leave the rest to you.

## Using Screen Capture

With Windows, using the <Print Screen> key sends information from the current screen display to the clipboard. Used on its own, it sends the whole screen display as a graphic image. If the <Alt> key is also depressed, it only sends the current window. Some of the graphics in this book were captured in this way.

These screen capture images can be loaded into Paint, edited, and then either saved as files, or used in a word processor or WordPad.

We will step through an example of this. First click the START button to display its menu and then press the <Print Screen> key. This sends a screen image to the clipboard.

Open a **New** file in the Paint program, use the **Edit**, **Paste** command and click on the Rectangle select Toolbar button. The screen image should now be loaded in Paint, use the scroll bars to move to the bottom left corner of the image. Select the menu area, as shown below, by clicking the cross hair pointer on one corner, dragging the dotted frame to the diagonal corner and clicking again.

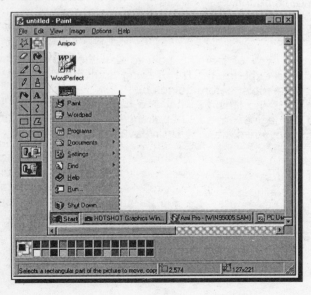

Now action the **Edit**, **Cut**, command to place the menu image on the clipboard. We also want to save it as a file for later on, so use the **Edit**, **Copy To** command and save the image with the name 'Menu example' in the same folder we used for the WordPad files earlier - C:\Program files\ Accessories.

## Embedding a Picture into WordPad:

Embedding a picture or a drawing into WordPad is similar to copying, but with the important advantage that you can actually edit an embedded object from within WordPad.

To embed our Paint image, first open WordPad, and if you saved our last memo example, open it. If not, just use an empty document. Press the <Ctrl+End> keys to jump to the end of the memo, add the extra sentence shown on the next page. Press the <Enter> key twice to make some room at the bottom of the text and centre the cursor by clicking the Centre justification icon.

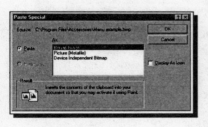

Then use the **Edit, Paste Special** command from the WordPad menu bar, accept the options shown here and press OK to place the graphic into the WordPad document, as shown on the next page.

What has happened here is that the graphic has been embedded in the WordPad document. If you double-click it, the WordPad window will change to a Paint window. You can then edit the image without leaving WordPad, and clicking outside the image will bring WordPad's features back.

The **Display as Icon** option embeds an icon in the destination document. Not much help in our example, but useful for embedding speech or movie clips in a document. Double-clicking the icon would then play the sound, or movie.

If you had chosen **Device Independent Bitmap** from the above box, the image would simply have been copied.

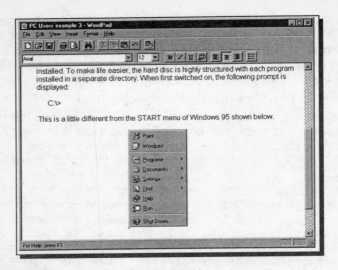

## Linking a Picture into WordPad:

Linking, the other main OLE feature, links files dynamically so that information held in one file is automatically updated when the information in the other file changes.

To link our graphic to WordPad, place the cursor in a new location and use WordPad's **Insert**, **Object** menu command, select 'Paintbrush Picture (Microsoft forgot to change this!) from the **Object Type** list and select the **Create from File** option.

Now locate the 'Menu example' file, using the **Browse** button facilities, or type in the path and filename. Finally, selecting **Link** and pressing **OK** will place a linked image of the file contents into the document.

When you double-click a linked image, its file is opened into a separate Paint window. Any changes made are saved in this file as well as being reflected in the document.

These are very clever features that can save a lot of time with full Windows applications. What we have covered here, should be a good grounding, but OLE (pronounced 'Oh Ley') can be quite complicated to understand. You must try these features for yourself, the time will be well spent.

# 6. MORE ACCESSORIES

## Windows 95 Multimedia

Multimedia is one of the buzz words of this decade as far as personal computers are concerned. What is it, do I hear some of you ask? Its simply the ability to play sound, and images (both still and moving) through a computer, usually from a CD-ROM disc. In other words, almost a cross between a PC and a TV!

Windows 95 has a multitude of 'hidden' features built into it to improve the PC's multimedia performance. These lead to a big improvement in both video and audio speed, quality and ease of use. As software developers bring out new programs to make use of these features we should see a transformation in this field.

Whether all the features described in the next few pages work on your PC will depend on your system. Most of them require at least a CD-ROM player, a sound card and speakers, to be fitted and correctly set up.

## Games:

We will not spend long on this topic, but many people only seem to have a PC to use it for playing games!

Our version of Windows 95 placed four games in the Games folder, under the Accessories group. One new one called Freecell, seems to be Patience based. The old Solitaire, designed to help with mouse skills, and Minesweeper are both still included. Hearts now has an option to connect to the Microsoft Hearts Network and play with other real people. Watch your phone bills though!

The best game of all we think, 3D Pinball, comes on the Microsoft Plus CD-ROM, an add-on pack to Windows 95.

All of these games come with quite good Help sections and we will leave it to you to explore them if you want.

## Media Player:

The Media Player, with the other features we will discuss, is found from the START menu by selecting, Programs, Accessories and then Multimedia.

As shown on the left, you must first select a type of file to play, from the **Device** menu.

If you have the Windows 95 CD-ROM, try the **Video for Windows** option, and look in the Videos sub-folder of the Funstuff folder. Double-click on one of the video files, maybe Goodtime, and then click the ▶ run button. Another way to run these demo videos is the 'Cool Video Clips' opening menu option from the CD-ROM itself.

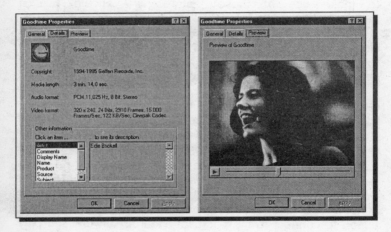

To see the properties of a video file, use a My Computer window to open the Videos folder, right-click the Goodtime file and select **Properties**. The opened sheet shows that this is a 23.1MB AVI video file.

Clicking the Details tab opens the left window shown above, with lots of information on the Edie Brickell video.

Clicking the Preview tab opens the video player, as shown on the right above. To start the video you must click the start arrow button ▶ below the screen. The slider to the right of the button, lets you move to different parts of the video.

To copy a multimedia file into a document is easy. Open the file from the Media Player, open the **Edit** menu, make your **Selection**, then specify any **Options** you want, then finally use the **Copy Object** command.

Next, open the document you want to copy the file to, click the cursor where you want it to appear and Paste it there. The example below shows an AVI video file and a WAV sound file both embedded in a Word for Windows document, but we could equally well have used WordPad.

## CD-ROM Player:

Cd player

Those of you that like to have music while you work, should love the CD-ROM player packaged with Windows 95.

To run it, select CD Player from the Multimedia sub-group of the START menu. This is a must for a Shortcut on the desktop, if you haven't mastered that technique yet, you should have done! The next page shows what the player looks like. To see what all the buttons do, read the pop-up that appears when you move the pointer over them.

It is well worth spending some time entering the details of your favourite music CD-ROMS with the **Disc**, **Edit Play List** option, while the particular disc is actually playing.

This not only lists the track details as they play, but lets you jump to a particular named one, to select a particular play order, or even to prevent a 'hated' track from playing at all. The Help system covers this quite well.

When you next play that disc all the details are remembered and are there for you to use.

## Sound Recorder:

We were not able to get the recorder to actually record anything, obviously our sound card settings were wrong.

Having said that, we found this accessory very useful for playing existing (WAV) sound files, and also for editing them.

You open it from the Multimedia START menu group. Use the **File**, **Open** menu command and look in the Media sub-folder of Windows. There should be half a dozen .WAV files in it. In our example above we selected 'The Microsoft Sound'. The controls are the same as with other multimedia players. Clicking the ▣ play button should play the 6.12 second sound - gripping?

The **Effects** menu lets you 'play around' with the sound, and the **Edit** menu lets you insert and mix other sound files into the loaded one, and delete parts of it.

Try out any changes you make by playing the file. If you want to keep the changes, make sure you save them before you quit the recorder.

# The Notepad

Notepad is now a 32-bit application, with long filename support. Apart from that, it appears very much the same. For new Windows users, it is a text editor which you can use to write short notes, or create and edit batch files. You can use Notepad to read and edit text files such as the various .TXT files supplied with Windows.

To see Notepad in operation, click its entry in the Accessories group of programs in the START menu, then select the **File, Open** command and look in the Windows folder of whatever drive it was installed on, probably C. There should be about a dozen text files (TXT) there just waiting to be opened. Double-click at the filename **Readme**.

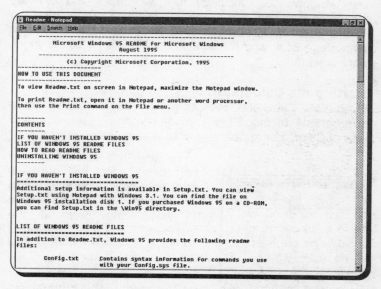

It is worth reading this file, particularly if you are experiencing difficulties while installing or running Windows 95.

## Notepad's Edit Features:

Although Notepad is not as powerful as WordPad, it has some interesting features, such as the ability to turn on word wrap which causes words that will not fit within its page margins to be placed on the next line automatically. You can turn word wrap on by selecting the **Edit, Word Wrap** command.

Another Notepad feature is the **Select All** option from the **Edit** menu which allows you to highlight a whole document at a stroke in order to, say, copy it onto the Clipboard.

Notepad supports the usual edit features which are useful when working with files, such as cut, copy, paste, and delete, all of which are options of the **Edit** menu.

You can even use Notepad to search and find text, by selecting the **Search, Find** command. Once the text is found, pressing **F3** finds the next occurrence.

## The Calculator

The Windows 95 Calculator has two faces; the ordinary calculator that can add, subtract, multiply, divide, take the square root of a number, find its reciprocal, or find a percentage of it, and the scientific calculator which is much more powerful.

### Starting the Calculator:

To start the Calculator, click its entry in the Accessory group of programs of the START menu. Normally, the standard view of Calculator appears on your screen, as shown here.

To use the calculator, you can either type the numbers and arithmetic operators from the keyboard, or use the mouse to point and click at the numbers and operators displayed in the calculator window. Obviously, if you wish to find the inverse of a number or its square root, you must use the Calculator keys as these operators are not on the keyboard. To find out the use of any particular key, right-click it and click on the **What's This?** button that opens. A short, but very adequate, description of the key function will display.

## The Calculator Memory:

The Calculator has four memory keys situated on the left-side of its window. Going from top to bottom, their functions are as follows:

| Key | Function |
|-----|----------|
| MC | Clears memory of stored values. |
| MR | Recalls stored values from memory to display. |
| MS | Stores the current displayed value in memory. |
| M+ | Adds the display value to a value in memory. |

## The Scientific Calculator:

You can access the scientific calculator by selecting the **View, Scientific** command from the menu bar. This is an altogether more complicated looking beast, as shown below:

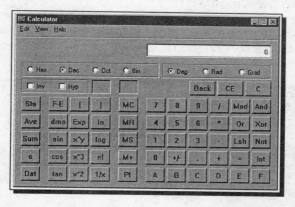

Obviously you will only need to use the scientific calculator if you already know how to use one. For this very reason we will not waste space and time explaining more complicated mathematical concepts.

You can transfer the results of any calculation from the Calculator's display to the Clipboard by selecting the **Edit, Copy** command, and then Paste them into an application.

## The Font Manager

Fonts

It is much easier to keep track of the fonts on your computer with Windows 95. The Fonts icon, located in the Control Panel, opens a special folder which holds all the fonts on your computer. To see what any particular font looks like, all you have to do is double-click its icon in this folder and an example window opens, as shown in the screen dump below.

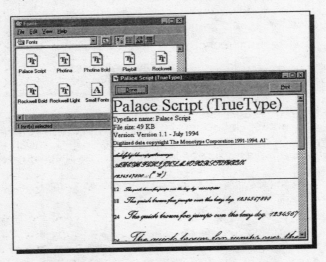

Many Windows programs add new fonts when they are installed, if you don't keep track of these, you can end up with a hard disc full of fonts you never use.

The **View** menu of the Fonts folder has several unusual options, as shown on the left. **List Fonts By Similarity**, groups your fonts on their similarity to a chosen one. You can then decide if there is any duplication. **Hide Variations (Bold, Italic, etc.)** reduces the list, so that it only holds one example from each font grouping. Select any fonts you don't need and use the **File**, **Delete** command.

## Character Map

A useful feature retained from Windows 3.x is the Character Map, shown open below. This should be found in the START menu Accessories group. You use this facility from your

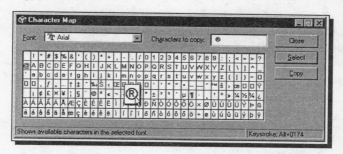

applications. When you need a particular special character, such as the 'registered sign ®' above, open the Character Map, select the **Font**, and look for that character. With high resolution monitors the characters are a little on the small side, so the one immediately under the pointer is automatically enlarged when the left mouse button is depressed.

When you find the character you want, click the **Select** button, which places it in the **Characters to copy** box. When you have all you want in this box, clicking the **Copy** button will copy them to the clipboard. Now, return to your application, make sure the insertion point is in the correct position and paste the characters there.

If you are observant, you may have noticed the message **Keystroke: Alt+0174** in the bottom right hand corner of the above window. This is the keyboard code of the highlighted character.

Another way to enter the character into your Windows application is to hold the <Alt> key down and enter that number from the right hand number key pad on your keyboard. When you release the <Alt> key the character should be placed at the insertion point. This only works, of course, if you have the <Num Lock> key active, otherwise you are not entering numbers from the key pad, but screen movement controls!

# 7. WINDOWS COMMUNICATIONS

To be able to communicate electronically with the rest of the World most users will need a modem connected, both to their PC, and to an active telephone line. This is a device that converts data so that it can be transmitted over the telephone system. Installing such a modem is quite easy with Windows 95, using the Add New Hardware Wizard described briefly in Chapter 4.

## Modem Properties

Before using your modem you must check to ensure it is correctly configured. To do this, double-click the Modems icon in the Control Panel. If Windows finds that no modem has been installed, it will step you through the process, using the relevant parts of the Add New Hardware Wizard. Otherwise it will open the Modems Properties sheet shown below.

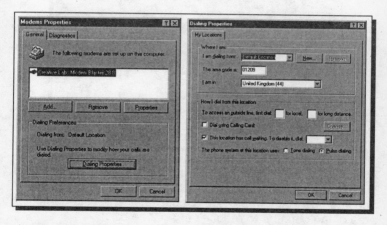

Clicking the **Properties** button will let you check the set up of your modem. If you do not understand the settings it would be best to accept the default ones. They will usually work.

The window above, on the right, is opened with the **Dialing Properties** button. Complete the options here for your PC, and maybe for different mobile PC locations.

## Microsoft Exchange

To use e-mail and send faxes from your PC, you can use the Microsoft Exchange provided, or buy suitable proprietary software.

To add Microsoft Exchange to your set-up (if it is not there already) use the Add/Remove Programs sheet, opened from the Control Panel, as described on page 65. If you have a CD-ROM version of Windows 95 you can also start this operation from the disc's opening menu, by selecting the Add/Remove Software option. The Inbox Setup Wizard is opened, as shown below.

To send and receive electronic mail over a modem, you must make an arrangement with a commercial server. There are quite a few around now, and most have Internet options. Try and find one that can provide a local service in your particular area of the country, to reduce your phone bills.

Once you have taken a subscription to such a service, you should be provided with all the necessary information to enter in the Inbox Setup Wizard, or better still, with alternative software!

When you are ready to complete this Wizard operation, just double-click the Inbox icon, which should now be on your desktop.

## HyperTerminal

HyperTerminal also allows you to connect your computer to other computers in different locations, so that you can interchange information. You could, for example, search a library catalogue, or browse through the offerings of a bulletin board.

Before you can connect to an outside service, you need to know their communications settings. For example, you need to know the settings for 'maximum speed', 'data bits', 'stop bits', and 'parity', though most of these can be safely assumed to be the same as the default values offered by HyperTerminal. Finally, before you can make the connection, you might need your credit card and to know a password or two, as these services are not free.

### Starting HyperTerminal:

To start HyperTerminal, click the START button, point to Programs, Accessories, and then click HyperTerminal.

This opens the window shown here, which is set to Large Icons. As you can see, it gives access to several mail services, such as CompuServe. If you want to subscribe to any of them, that is the easy way to start.

Double-click the Hypertrm icon to start HyperTerminal itself. If this is the first time that you have accessed HyperTerminal, the colourful window shown below is opened to help you make your first connection.

Every call connection in HyperTerminal can be named and saved with an icon, so that in future it is very easy to re-call the same number.

We have given ours the rather stupid name of 'First connection'. Selecting **OK** opens the next window, in which you enter the phone number of the site you want to connect to. Make sure the modem is correctly selected and press **OK** again. The Connect window, shown in the composite below, is the last stage.

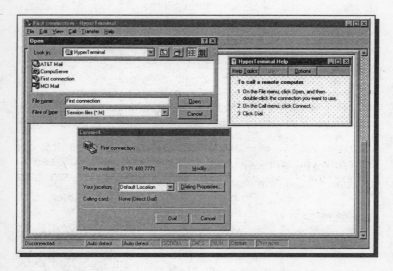

To use the default modem settings, just click the **Dial** button to attempt a connection. To call the same number again in the future, use the **File**, **Open** command and double-click its name in the Open dialogue box, as shown above.

For more information about how to use HyperTerminal, click its Help menu and browse through the Contents section. For Windows 95 this is quite detailed.

### Specifying Communications Settings:
If you have trouble getting through, you may need to fine tune the settings. Any time a call is 'open' in the HyperTerminal window use the **File**, **Properties** menu command to change call settings, or if necessary, to **Configure** the modem so that it speaks the same 'language' as the remote system. This opens the tabbed dialogue box shown on the facing page.

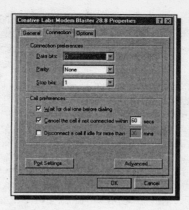

Normally, you will find that the default parameters in this are the ones you want to use. However, in case you need to change them, we list below some alternatives and their usage.

| Option | Result |
|--------|--------|
| Maximum speed | Specifies the transmission, or baud, rate at which your system sends and receives data. The type of modem attached to your system determines the rate. |
| Data Bits | Specifies the number of data bits (binary digits) that each data packet, sent or received, contains. |
| Stop Bits | Specifies the time between transmitted characters. |
| Parity | Allows you to specify how the receiving computer verifies the accuracy of the data you are sending. |
| Flow Control | Allows you to specify what HyperTerminal should do if its buffer fills up during data |

reception. Xon/Xoff tells HyperTerminal to pause when the
buffer fills, and to send a message to the remote system
when ready to receive more
data.

## Setting Terminal Preferences:

The terminal type used by the destination site will determine
the terminal type which should be used for a connection.
HyperTerminal supports several common types, but in most
cases the Auto detect option will sort this out automatically.

To make a manual selection, click the Settings tab of the
New Connection Properties sheet, as shown below on the
left, with the **Emulation** list open.

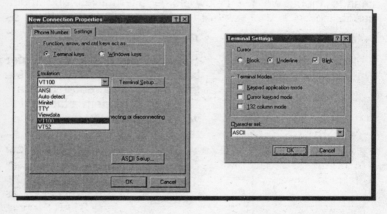

Select the correct terminal option and then click **Terminal
Setup** to set its preferences. The set-up shown on the right
above is for the VT100 selected in the main settings sheet.

## File Transfer Protocols:

Before you can send or receive files using HyperTerminal's
**Transfer** command, you need to specify the transfer
protocol. The type of files you send or receive will be either
text or binary files.

**Text files:** are normally prepared with a text editor or a word processor, such as WordPad or Notepad, but saved unformatted. This means that files are saved in ASCII format with only a few formatting codes such as carriage returns and linefeeds. You can select **ASCII Setup** on the New Connection Properties sheet to control transmission of this type of file.

**Binary files:** are normally program files which contain characters from both the ASCII and the extended ASCII character sets.

HyperTerminal supports many of the most popular protocols; which one to use depends on the receiving site. Zmodem is now supported and should be used whenever possible as it gives the fastest transfer rates and remembers its place if your transmission is interrupted.

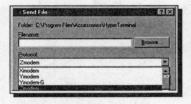

You select the protocol as part of the **Send File**, or **Receive File** operation, started from the **Transfer** menu, as shown in the window alongside.

## The Phone Dialer

If you have the facility to connect a normal telephone to your modem, you should be able to use the Phone Dialer to easily dial and log all your calls. If installed, you should find the program in the Accessories sub-group of the START menu.

To make a call, simply enter the number in the text box and click the **Dial** button. The down arrow will open a list of most recently used numbers.

To enter numbers into the Speed Dial option buttons, use the **Edit**, **Speed Dial** menu command, click one of the 8 buttons, type its name and then the required number. When set up, you just click one of these to dial its number.

## Towards the Mobile Office

Several of Windows 95's features are geared to making life a little easier for those that use computers on the move.

### Dial-Up Networking:

With Dial-Up Networking, you can access shared information on another computer, even if your computer is not connected to the network. To do this you must dial directly to the network server, which controls the resources of the network.

If you have a computer at home, you can dial in to your office network server and connect to your work computer. Obviously, both your computer at home and

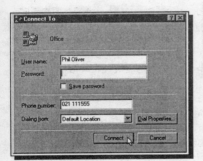

the network server at work must have modems installed.

To start the Dial-Up Networking set-up wizard, double-click the My Computer icon, and then double-click the Dial-Up Networking icon, if it is there. If it is not, you will need to install it from the Windows 95 system discs, or CD-ROM.

The Wizard steps you through the process of making your first connection. After that, when you open the Dial-Up Networking window, there is an icon for every connection made, and one to help you make a new connection.

In our example above, to connect to our office, we would simply double-click the Office icon, enter the **Password** and click the **Connect** button. We could make the procedure even easier by placing a Shortcut on the desktop, as described in an earlier chapter.

## Using a Briefcase:

You can use the Briefcase feature to keep your copies of files updated when you work on them away from your PC. The two main uses are if you work with a mobile when away from the office, or if you transport files home in the evening on floppy discs to work on your own PC. Sooner, or later, you end up with the situation that the two sets of files are different and you don't know which to use.

My Briefcase

Hopefully, you should have a My Briefcase icon on your desktop, but this will be the case only if you chose the Portable option during Windows 95 set-up, or if you chose the Custom option and then specified installing Briefcase. In fact, we had to re-install Windows 95 to find it. It did not appear for us as an option in the Add/Remove Programs sheet, opened from the Control Panel, as described in the Help window.

To use Briefcase with a mobile, you connect both computers and drag the files from their folders on your main computer to the Briefcase folder icon on your mobile. When you next return to the office, after working on the files, reconnect to your main computer, open the Briefcase and click **Update All** in the **Briefcase** menu to automatically update the files on your main computer with the modified ones in your Briefcase. Sounds a little complicated, but it's not really.

To use a Briefcase with a floppy, you first move the Briefcase icon onto the floppy disc, then you drag the files you want to take home, from your main computer to the Briefcase icon on the floppy.

Take the floppy home and burn the midnight oil, using the files from the Briefcase. No need to copy them anywhere, but obviously make sure you save your work back to the Briefcase, before calling it a day.

When back in the office, open your floppy, right-click on the Briefcase icon and select **Update All**, as shown above.

111

Now to the clever bit. The window below will open, listing any files that have been amended.

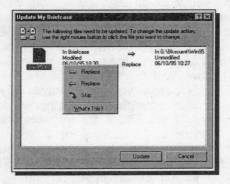

In our case, there was only one file. If you are happy with the suggested course of action in this window, click the **Update** button. If not, you can right-click a file name and change the action, as shown above. The **What's This** option gives you some help, if you need it.

**NOTE:** - It is essential that you close the Briefcase located on a removable disc, before you actually remove the disc from your PC. This is to ensure that the Briefcase database is updated, otherwise you will be in danger of losing data. If you are careless here, Windows tries to warn you with the message shown. If you still ignore this, you get a horrific 'blue screen DOS type' message that should wake you up!

# 8. SYSTEM TOOLS

Windows 95, as you would expect, comes equipped with a full range of system utility programs so that you can maintain your PC's set-up as easily as possible. By default, access to all these tools is from the START menu, using the route, Programs, Accessories, System Tools.

## The Backup Program

Backup

Backing up both your system set-up and data files from hard disc to another storage medium, is something that everyone should do on a regular basis. Hard discs can 'crash' (though not as often these days as they used to) and your PC could be stolen, or lost in a fire, or flood. Any of these events would cause a serious data loss, unless you had backed it all up, and stored it safely.

Microsoft have commissioned a new 32-bit Backup utility which, unfortunately, is not compatible with any earlier versions. If you have any files archived with a previous Backup, or MSBackup version, make sure you keep the older DOS utilities, or you won't be able to Restore them!

When opened for the first time Backup displays a window telling you about a Full System Backup-set it has prepared. Read this and click the box in its bottom corner, or you will have to put up with it again! Next on our PC, was a long message about tape drives. If you do not use one, click **OK** to continue.

### Making a Backup:

We will step through the procedure of backing up, and then restoring, a folder of files. You should then be happy to carry on by yourself.

When Backup is open, there are three tabs across the top of the window. These determine what mode the program is in, Backup, Restore or Compare.

In our example, on the next page, we wanted to back up some of the files for this book, which were stored in the Win95 folder, shown in the left side Explorer type window.

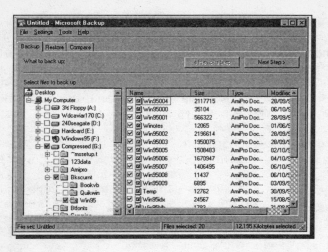

First open the tree structure by clicking the + signs, until the folder wanted is visible. To select all the files in a folder you click the small box to its left, which will grey it. To select, or de-select, individual files, tick in their boxes in the right hand pane. Check the **Settings**, **Options** dialogue box to set the type of back up wanted and the correct paths, etc., and then click the **Next Step** button.

In the next window, select your floppy drive to place its drive letter in the **Selected device...** box, place a labelled disc in the drive and click on **Start Backup**. Enter a name to

describe the back up, that will mean something to you in the future, in our case we used 'Win 95 book files', and click **OK**.

The window shown here displays to keep you informed during the process. Place discs in the drive when asked. In our case the 20 files of 12.195MB took 4.14 minutes to back up and actually fitted

on two 1.4MB floppy discs. In other words the files were well compressed, with many embedded graphics the ratio was about 10:1.

## Restoring your Files:

To restore files that have been previously backed up, place the first disc of the set in the disc drive, click the Restore tab and select the floppy drive in the **Restore from** window. This should bring up the name of the back up set in the right window pane, as shown below.

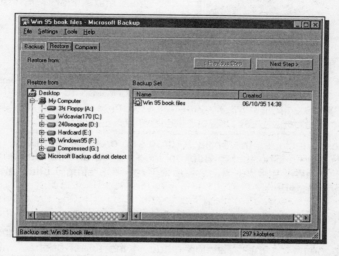

Use the **Settings**, **Options**, menu command and select the **Restore** tab to select where to restore the files and other settings.

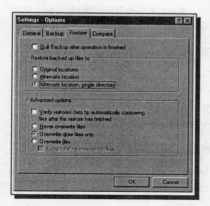

In our example, to the left, we have chosen the **Alternate location, single directory** option as the destination for our restored files. In other words they will be restored to a single folder, that we will specify, instead of to their original drive and folders. The other options control whether the Backup program closes when the

restore operation is finished and sets priorities for file overwriting, etc.

If you opted to restore to a different destination, the next window will allow you to select the drive and folder, and then click **OK** to start the process.

## Using Compare:

The Compare tab option of Backup lets you compare a back up set with the original files. The operation is almost the same as with restore, except that you must start with the last disc of a back up set in your floppy drive.

Backup includes the ability to drag and drop file and back up sets onto a 'Shortcut to Backup' icon placed on your desktop. This makes starting a backup operation a simple **click and drag** procedure.

## Types of Backups:

The Backup program will perform two types of back ups, depending on the selection made in the sheet opened with the **Settings**, **Options** menu command, with the **Backup** tab active:

**Full**        Backs up all selected files, regardless of whether or not they have changed since the last backup, and lowers the archive flags. This is the default option.

**Incremental**  Backs up all selected files that have changed since the last full or incremental backup, and lowers the archive flags. This type is for the partial backups in your backup cycle, if you work with different files each day. With this method it is important to save all incremental backup sets between full backups.

## A Backup Strategy:

Hopefully you should by now be completely sold on the Backup program we have been using. It is only any use though if you use it systematically and with discipline.

We suggest the following full and incremental back up procedure may be useful to you if you generally work with different files, and create new ones, each day.

You have to keep the full backup set with all incremental backup sets. This is important since each incremental backup records a different increment of changes. Also make sure the settings option **Always erase on floppy disk backups** is **NOT** selected.

To use the incremental backup procedure:

1       Perform a full backup of all your data files.

2       Each day, before you switch off, perform an incremental backup. Use the same floppy disc until it fills up, then start another disc.

3       Save all your floppy discs from the cycle until after you have performed the next full backup.

4       Perform the next full backup, maybe after one or two weeks, **using different discs**.

5       Perform the daily incremental backups as in step 2, and repeat the cycle.

It is also important to look after your backup disc sets. Label them carefully and write the set name on them all. Also make sure you keep each complete set together, and if your data is very important, keep the backup sets well away from the computer, and from each other.

With a little bit of discipline and a lot of Backup you should never have serious data loss problems, even if your hard disc explodes, or someone takes a liking to your computer.

## ScanDisk

ScanDisk is a disc checking and repair tool designed to help check the integrity of discs and to fix any problems that are found. It is a graphical application that runs under Windows,

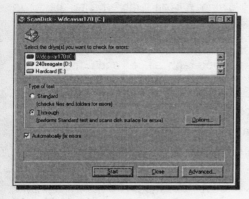

which you should find from the START menu, in the System Tools sub group of Accessories.

As shown on the left, you can run a **Standard** scan, in which ScanDisk only checks the files on your system for errors, or a **Thorough** scan, which checks both the files and the disc surface for errors. If the **Automatically fix errors** option is checked, any errors found will be sorted out.

## Defragmenting your Hard Discs

The Disk Defragmenter optimises a hard disc by rearranging the data on it to eliminate unused spaces, which speeds up access to the disc by Windows 95 operations. As is also the

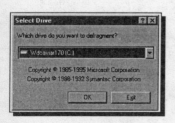

case with ScanDisk, you don't need to exit a running application to run the Disk Defragmenter. Choose which drive to defragment in the Select Drive box, shown here, and you can defragment it in the background while working with another application. You can watch the progress of the operation, or display it in minimal status.

You should get in the habit of checking and optimising your hard discs regularly with these two tools.

118

## Disc Compression

Disc compression - the ability to greatly increase the storage capacity of your discs with no extra hardware cost, has been around for several years now, and seems to be fairly well accepted.

Windows 95 includes DriveSpace disc compression which is compatible with the DoubleSpace and DriveSpace compression provided with MS-DOS 6.0 and 6.2. If your system uses either of these methods, you don't need to take any special actions when you install Windows 95. Your compressed discs will be 'taken over as they are'.

### How it Works:

DriveSpace compresses the files in a drive by a default factor of between 1.5 and 2.5 and hence lets you store much more on that drive. When you use files on the compressed drive, DriveSpace transparently uncompresses them, so that they can be accessed; and then re-compresses them when they are saved again.

This decompression and compression of files is carried on automatically in the background. This can, however, lead to a slowing down of operations, especially when moving files from one compressed drive to another. If you need to do that, we suggest you make a cup of coffee.

When DriveSpace first compresses a drive, it sets up a hidden file on an uncompressed part of the drive, which is then treated as a new logical drive. Thus for every hard drive you compress you acquire another drive letter.

When you open DriveSpace, a window like the one shown here, gives you the choice of compressing your hard disc

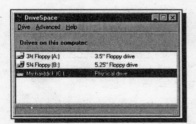

drives as well as any removable floppy drives on your system.

To compress a drive, simply double-click its entry on the list. This opens the Compress a Drive dialogue box, shown on the next page.

119

This box shows the amount of free space on the selected drive available before compression and the estimated situation after compression. Clicking the **Options** button lets you fine tune the procedure, and when you are ready, clicking the **Start** button begins the process.

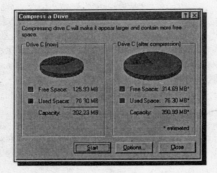

# 9. USING MS-DOS AND DOS PROGRAMS

If you are an experienced PC user, you may well prefer to do much of your work by entering instructions at the DOS command line, or prompt. Windows 95 still lets you do this. In fact this way of working is much easier now than in previous versions of DOS.

For this book we have assumed that if you want to use this method of working you will already be familiar with DOS commands, switches, filters and batch files, etc. If not, we suggest you use the methods described in earlier chapters. A full listing of the commands available is included in the next chapter. There are a few new ones, many have been made obsolete, but they all support Windows 95 32-bit features and long file names.

## Using the Run Window

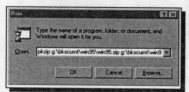

With Windows 95, the easiest way to issue a single DOS command, that involves running a program, is in the **Run** window, opened from the START menu.

Its big advantage is that all your previous commands are remembered. Clicking the down arrow, opens a small 'database' of your most used commands, including path and file names, etc. The command itself is actioned in a 'one off' DOS window, as shown below.

When you have read the result in this window you have to close it, by clicking the X close button, in the top right hand corner.

## Using an MS-DOS Window

To open an MS-DOS window, click the START button, point to **Programs** and click **MS-DOS Prompt** from the cascade menu. Better still, make a Shortcut on the desktop, and in future just double-click this to open a window like that below.

You can action any DOS commands you like in this window. To view the toolbar, if it is not showing, click the MS-DOS icon in the title bar to open the command menu, and then click the **Toolbar** toggle option.

To switch between a window and full screen, click the Full screen toolbar icon. The <Alt+Enter> key combination also toggles between these two modes

To quit the MS-DOS window and return to normal Windows 95 operation, click the X Close button of a window, or type exit at the command prompt.

## Using the Toolbar:

The toolbar is a very useful feature of an MS-DOS window. You can mark text and copy it to the Windows clipboard, or paste from the clipboard. You can also carry out these functions from the Command menu, by selecting **Edit**, **Mark**, **Edit**, **Copy**, or **Edit**, **Paste**.

122

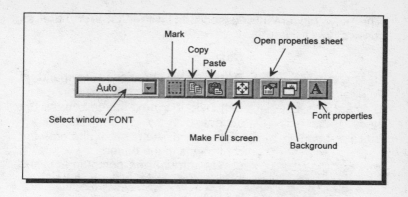

Mark
Copy
Paste
Open properties sheet
Select window FONT
Make Full screen
Background
Font properties
Auto

## The DOSKEY Utility:

This utility, when loaded into your system, allows you to recall the most recently entered DOS commands at the system prompt, for subsequent use, which can save you a lot of retyping. You will find that learning to use DOSKEY will be extremely useful to you if you use the command prompt very much.

DOSKEY is an example of a TSR (terminate-and-stay-resident) program. Once a TSR is loaded into memory, it stays in the background without interfering with the other programs you are running. To load DOSKEY into RAM, type

```
DOSKEY
```

at the command prompt in a DOS window and press <Enter>. If you are going to use DOSKEY frequently, you should include the command in your AUTOEXEC.BAT file, which loads the program automatically every time you switch on your system.

Once DOSKEY is in memory, every time you type a command at the system prompt, the command is stored in the DOSKEY buffer, which is 512 bytes long.

To recall the most recently executed DOS command, simply press the <↑> key. Each time this is pressed, the next most recently executed DOS command is displayed.

When the required command is displayed at the prompt, pressing the <←> or <→> keys allows you to edit the command, while pressing <Enter> re-executes it.

123

The key movements associated with DOSKEY, are as follows:

| Key | Result |
| --- | --- |
| ↑ | Displays the previous command in the buffer list. |
| ↓ | Displays the next command in the buffer list. |
| F7 | Displays a numbered list of the commands in the buffer. |
| F8 | Cycles through the commands in the buffer that start with a letter you specify. |
| F9 | Prompts you for the number of the stored command in the list (obtained by using the F7 function key). |
| Page Up | Displays the first command in the buffer list. |
| Page Down | Displays the last command in the buffer list. |
| Esc | Clears the command at the prompt. |
| Alt+F7 | Clears the list of commands from the buffer. |

## The DOS Editor

Windows 95 includes a new version of the MS-DOS text editor, EDIT.COM. Users of MS-DOS will find the Edit program very familiar, but it has several improvements.

- Edit is smaller and faster than its predecessor.

- You can open up to nine files at the same time, split the screen between two files, and easily copy and paste information between them.

- You can open files as large as 4 MB.

- Edit supports long filenames and allows you to open filenames and navigate through the directory structure just as you can in the rest of Windows 95.

The editor is opened, as one would expect from its name, by typing EDIT at the command prompt.

```
ECHO OFF
VERIFY OFF
PATH C:\WINDOWS;C:\WINDOWS\COMMAND;C:\DOS;C:\BATCH;C:\UTILS;C:\pkware;G:\WP60
SET TEMP=C:\windows\TEMP
SET TMP=C:\windows\TEMP
SET TZ=GMT+1BST
SET PC=d:\POSTCODE
PROMPT $P$G
C:\WINDOWS\COMMAND\doskey
mode con codepage prepare=((850) C:\WINDOWS\COMMAND\ega.cpi)
mode con codepage select=850
keyb uk,,C:\WINDOWS\COMMAND\keyboard.sys
```

We will leave it up to you to explore this new addition to your
MS-DOS environment. To help you on your way, the **F1** key
will open a list of all the cursor movement, editing, and
function commands, as well as some shortcut keys.

## DOS Program Properties

With earlier versions of Windows you had to make and edit a
PIF (program information file) for a particular DOS program,
to control how it functioned under Windows. This procedure
was not understood, or used, by many people, so most DOS
programs wouldn't work properly for them under Windows.

With Windows 95, PIF files still exist, but you don't need to
worry about them. They are either provided already, or made
up by Windows from an existing file, or from settings you
easily control, in an applications Properties sheet.

Every object in Windows 95 has a set of properties, and
with MS-DOS based (rather than Windows based) programs,
this sheet very strictly controls how the program will function
when run in Windows 95.

The easy way to open an application's property sheet is to
right-click the application icon in a folder and select
**Properties** from the opened object menu.

To demonstrate this, we will look through all the properties
of the DOS program COMMAND.COM, which is in the
Windows folder and is the program run when you click
**MS-DOS Prompt** from the START cascade menu.

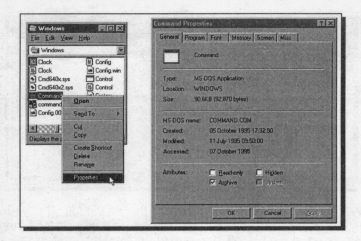

The opening sheet, shown above, gives the file's details and allows you to set its attributes. Clicking the Program tab, opens the next sheet, shown on the left below.

Click this to either set up this program to have exclusive use of your computer (MS-DOS mode) or enable Windows-based programs to be run in addition to this program.

To find out more detail on any option, click the **?** window button and then click the query pointer on the item. A description box is opened, like the one above, which opens when the **Advanced** button is clicked. The Advanced Program Settings are shown on the right below.

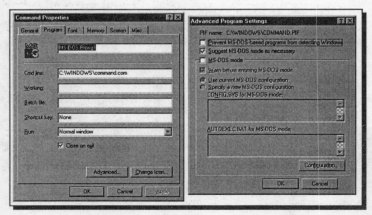

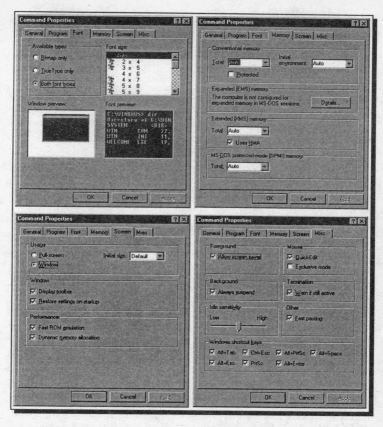

Spending some time working through these sheets will ensure that your MS-DOS applications work the way you want them to, when run under Windows 95.

## Running DOS Programs

To help ensure as many MS-DOS based programs as possible work properly with Windows 95, the file APPS.INF is provided, containing program settings for many popular MS-DOS applications. These settings are based on test results and specify the special settings necessary to allow the application to run under Windows 95.

When you attempt to run an MS-DOS application, Windows first looks for its PIF. If one doesn't exist for that application, the APPS.INF file is searched. If the application is listed, the system reads the contents and creates a PIF that is used to run the program.

## Real Mode:

To provide support for 'rogue' MS-DOS–based applications that work only under MS-DOS (requiring full access to the system components and resources), Windows 95 provides **MS-DOS mode**. This is the equivalent of running the application in real-mode MS-DOS.

In this mode, Windows 95 removes itself from memory (except for a small section) and provides the application with full access to all the resources of the computer. Not many applications need to run in single MS-DOS application mode, but one of them is MSBackup, provided with MS-DOS 6.

To set up a program to run in this mode, you select **MS-DOS mode** on the Advanced Program Settings sheet (as shown at the bottom of page 126) for the application. On this sheet you can also specify a CONFIG.SYS or AUTOEXEC.BAT file to run for the application.

When the application in then run, Windows closes all running tasks, (after getting your 'permission'), configures the PC to use the CONFIG.SYS and AUTOEXEC.BAT files for the session, restarts the computer, loads a real-mode copy of MS-DOS, and runs the application.

When you close the MS-DOS application, Windows 95 restarts as normal. This is quite a performance and if you have a slow PC it is very time consuming. But it does mean that most MS-DOS programs can be run under Windows 95.

## More on Long Filenames

The use of long filenames, of up to 255 characters, allows you to use more user-friendly filenames, but what happens to them when you return to an older application that does not support long filenames? Windows 95 actually keeps track of two filenames, the long one you provide, and one in the old MS-DOS 8.3 format which it 'makes up' for compatibility with existing programs that can only use 8.3 filenames.

Long filenames are supported by extending the MS-DOS FAT file system and using previously reserved areas to add directory entries to look after the long filename information.

If a file, or directory, on a disc that has a long filename is viewed on a computer that is not running Windows 95, only its 8.3 filename is seen. The example below shows the directory of a disc with both 8.3 and long filenames.

As you can see, the listing on the left is in 8.3 format, and their corresponding long names are shown on the right. The last two directories listed above are actually the only two that have been given long names, the others were all pre Windows 95.

If you look carefully, you should be able to work out how their corresponding 8.3 names were made up. Windows takes the first 6 characters of the long name, adds a '~' character and then the digit 1. The next long name it encounters with the same first 6 characters, it will add the digit 2, and so on.

This is fine for most cases, but can be dangerous. Imagine a directory of report files you have named as follows:

| Long filename | 8.3 Name |
|---|---|
| Report for January 1995 | Report~1 |
| Report for February 1995 | Report~2 |
| etc. | |

Fine for the first 9 files, but confusion from then on. So, if you will ever need to use your files in an application that only supports the old format, you must choose your long names with care to help the system out.

***Another word of warning:*** Most file utility programs not designed for Windows 95 will destroy any long filenames they encounter. Not surprising really, as they haven't been written to expect them. The moral is to scrap all such programs.

## Wildcard Characters

You are probably aware of the two Wildcard characters, * and ?. When used in a command line, * can be substituted for any number of characters in a filename mask, and ? for just a single character. Thus *.EXE, means all files with the extension of EXE, and *.E?? means all files with a 3 character extension beginning with E.

The use of the * Wildcard has been extended in Windows 95, to make it more powerful when used with long filenames.

You can now use more than one * in a name mask. The following is now legal in Windows 95

```
Del *Jan*
```

This command would delete all the files in the current directory with 'Jan' anywhere in their name. So be aware!

# 10. WINDOWS 95 DOS COMMANDS

The following is a list of all the native Windows 95 commands which now take advantage of the 32-bit operating system. Most of them can be run from a DOS window, or file. They are labelled internal or external, with external commands being accessible to the user only if the full filespec (drive and path) is given to where the command file resides. External files can also be run from the Run command, the START menu and from Windows Explorer. Examples of command usage are given whenever possible.

Where '(high)' appears alongside a command its use causes reserved memory to be removed from the upper memory area (UMA), e.g. 'buffers and 'buffershigh'.

Windows 95 does not support the following commands:

append, assign, backup, comp, dosshell, edlin, expand, fasthelp, fastopen, graphics, graftabl, help, interlnk, intersvr, join, loadfix, memcard, memmaker, mirror, msav, msbackup, power, print, qbasic, recover, replace, restore, share, sizer, smartmon, tree, undelete, unformat, vsafe.

| *Command* | *Explanation* |
|---|---|
| attrib [filespec] | External - sets or resets the *read only* attribute & archive bit of a file, and displays the attributes of a file. |

Switches:
+a sets the archive bit of a file
−a clears the archive bit
+h sets the file as a hidden file
−h clears the hidden file attribute
+r sets read-only mode of a file
−r disables read-only mode
+s sets the file as a system file
−s clears the system file attribute
/s processes files in the current directory and all of its sub-directories.

Example: attrib +r filespec

| | |
|---|---|
| break | Internal - CONFIG.SYS - sets the Ctrl+Break, or the extended Ctrl+C checking. |
| | Example: break ON |
| buffers(high) | Internal - CONFIG.SYS - allocates memory for a specified number of disc buffers (1-99). |
| | Example: buffers=40,m |
| | where m is optional and specifies the number of the secondary buffer cache (0-8). |
| call | Internal - calls one batch file from another without exiting from the first one. |
| cd (or chdir) | Internal - changes the working directory to a different directory. |
| | Example: cd\wproc\docs |
| chcp [nnn] | Internal - selects current code page for as many devices as possible. Omitting *nnn* displays the current code page. |
| chkdsk [filespec] | External - analyses the directories, files, and File Allocation Table on the logged or designated drive and produces a status report. It also reports the volume, serial number and disc allocation units. Better to use Scandiskw from Windows |
| | Switches: |
| | /f fixes any problems found during the check |
| | /v causes the display of filespecs as they are being processed. |

Example: chkdsk a:/f/v

choice        External - prompts the user to make a choice in a batch file.

Switches:

/c:keys    specifies allowable keys in the prompt. When displayed, the keys will be followed by a question mark. If you don't specify the /c switch, choice uses YN as the default

/n         causes choice not to display the prompt. The text before the prompt is still displayed, however. If you specify the /n switch, the specified keys are still valid

/s         causes choice to be case sensitive

/t:c,nn    causes choice to pause for nn (0-99) seconds, before defaulting to a specified key, c.

cls          Internal - clears the screen.

command [filespec]    External - starts the command processor which is loaded into memory in two parts; the resident part and the transient part. If the transient part is overwritten by a program, it is reloaded.

Switches:

/c executes a following command

|  | /e specifies the environment size in bytes (160-32768, default = 160 bytes) |
|---|---|
|  | /k runs the specified command and keeps running |
|  | /p prohibits command.com from exiting to a higher level |
|  | /l specifies internal buffers length |
|  | /u specifies the input buffer length |
|  | /y steps through the batch program specified by /c or /k. |
| copy [filespec] | Internal - copies one or more files to specified disc. If preferred, copies can be given different names.

Switches:
/a indicates an ASCII text file
/b indicates a binary file
/v causes the verification of data written on the destination disc.

Example: copy *.exe a:/v

copies all files with the .exe extension to the a: drive with verification. |
| country | External - CONFIG.SYS - enables DOS to use country-specific conventions for displaying dates, times, and currency. |
| ctty | Internal - changes the standard I/O console to an auxiliary (aux) console, and vice versa.

Example: ctty aux

moves all input/output from the current device (console) to an aux port such as another terminal. |

The command *ctty con* moves I/O back to the console.

Valid values for the device parameter are prn, lpt1, lpt2, lpt3, con, aux, com1, com2, com3, and com4.

date
Internal - enters or changes the current date.

drvspace
External, Windows utility - sets-up or configures compressed drives.

debug
External - starts the debug program that allows you to create or edit executable files.

defrag
External, Windows utility - reorganises files on a disc to optimise performance.

del [filespec]
Internal - deletes all files with the designated filespec.

Switch:
/p displays filenames to confirm deletion.

Example: del a:\*.txt
deletes all .txt files from the root directory of the a: drive.

deltree
External - deletes a specified directory and all the files and subdirectories that might be in it.

Switch:
/y carries out the command without first prompting you for confirmation.

device(high)          Internal - loads a specified device driver into memory from within your CONFIG.SYS file.

dir [filespec]        Internal - lists files in a directory. Filespec specifies drive, directory, and/or files to list

Switches:

/a displays only the names of those directories and files with the attributes you specify.

For example: (– prefix means not)

a  files ready for archiving
d  directories
h  hidden files
r  read-only files
s  system files.

/b lists each directory name or file, one per line, (including the file extension), but no heading

/l displays unsorted directory and filenames in lower case

/o: controls the sort order in which a directory listing is displayed.

For example, (– prefix to reverse order)

a  by Last access date, earliest first
d  by date & time, earliest first
e  in alphabetical order by extension
g  with directories grouped before files
n  in alphabetical order
s  by size, smallest first.

| | |
|---|---|
| | /p displays the directory listing a page at a time |
| | /s lists every occurrence, in the specified directory and all sub-directories, of the specified filename |
| | /v displays the directory listing in verbose mode |
| | /w displays the directory listing in wide format. |
| diskcopy | External - copies the contents of the disc in the source drive to the disc in the destination drive |
| | Switches: |
| | /1 Copies only the first side |
| | /v verifies correct copying |
| | /m forces multi-pass copies using memory only. |
| dos | Internal - CONFIG.SYS - specifies that DOS should maintain a link to the upper memory area (UMA), load part of itself into high memory area (HMA), or both. |
| doskey | External - starts the doskey pro-gram which recalls DOS commands. |
| | Switches: |
| | /bufsize=  allows the specification of the buffer size to be used for storing com-mands. The default size is 512 bytes, while the minimum buffer size is 256 bytes |
| | /insert  switches on the 'insert' mode |

| | |
|---|---|
| /history | displays a list of all commands stored in memory |
| /macros | displays a list of all doskey macros |
| /overstrike | switches on the 'overstrike' mode |
| /echo | enables/disables (:on\|off) echo of macro expansions (default - on) |
| /file:name | specifies file containing a list of macros (name) |
| /keysize:n | sets size of keyboard type-ahead buffer to n (default n:15) |
| /line:n | sets maximum size of line edit buffer to n (default n:12) |
| /reinstall | installs a new copy of doskey and clears the buffer of the current copy. |
| | |
| drivparm | External - CONFIG.SYS - allows you to define parameters for devices such as disc and tape drives when you start your computer. |
| | |
| echo | Internal - sets Echo to on or off. |
| | |
| edit | External - activates a screen editor which is used to create or edit ASCII text files. |
| | |
| emm386 | External - enables or disables expanded memory support on a computer with an 80386 or higher processor. |
| | |
| erase | Internal - same as del command. |

| | |
|---|---|
| exit | Internal - exits the command processor and returns to a previous level. |
| expand | External - expands a compressed file. |
| fc [filespec] | External - compares two files and displays the differences between them. |

Switches:
/a abbreviates the output of an ASCII comparison to only the first and last line of each set of differences
/b compares binary files
/c ignores the case of letters
/l compares ASCII files line by line
/n displays the line numbers during an ASCII comparison
/t does not expand tabs to spaces
/w compresses tabs and spaces during the comparison.

| | |
|---|---|
| fcbs(high) | Internal - CONFIG.SYS - specifies the number of file control blocks (FCBs) that DOS can have open at the same time (1-255, default = 4). |
| fdisk | External - sets up and partitions the fixed disc for use with Windows 95. Cannot be used while Windows is running from the drive. |

Switch:
/status displays an overview of the partition information without starting Fdisk.

| files(high) | Internal - CONFIG.SYS - specifies the number of files that DOS can access at one time. |
| --- | --- |
| find [filespec] | External - searches for a specific string of text in a specified ASCII file or files. |

Switches:
- /c prints the count of lines containing the string
- /i search is insensitive to the case of letters
- /n precedes each occurrence with the relative line number in the file
- /v displays all lines not containing the specified string.

Example: find "lost words" chap1 searches for the string *lost words* (which must appear within full quotes) in the named file (chap1).

| for | Internal - repeats a command for each file in a set of files. |
| --- | --- |
| format [filespec] | External - formats the disc in the specified drive. |

Switches:
- /4 formats a double-sided disc with 40 tracks, 9 sectors per track for 360 KB in a high capacity (1.2 MB) disc drive
- /8 formats with 8 sectors per track
- /b reserves space for system files
- /f:size
  specifies the size of the disc to be formatted. Use one of the following values for size, which

specifies the capacity of the disc in Kbytes:

160, or 180, for single-sided, double-density 5¼" discs,
320, or 360, for double-sided, double-density 5¼" discs,
720 for double-sided, double-density 3½" discs,
1200, or 1.2, for double-sided, high-capacity 5¼" discs,
1440, or 1.44, for double-sided, high-capacity 3½" discs,
2880, or 2.88, for 2.88 MB, double-sided, 3½" discs.

/n  specifies the number of sectors per track, i.e. /n:9 for nine sectors
/q  performs a quick format
/s  copies the system files from the logged drive
/t  specifies the number of tracks, i.e. /t:40 for forty tracks
/v:label
    allows you to specify *label* without prompting after the formatting process.

Example: format a:/4/s

goto            Internal - jumps to a labelled line within the same batch file.

if              Allows conditional execution of commands within a batch file.

include         Internal - CONFIG.SYS - includes the contents of one configuration block within another.

141

| install | Internal - CONFIG.SYS - installs a memory-resident program into memory. |
|---|---|
| keyb [xx] | External - selects a special keyboard layout. Omitting **xx** returns the current status of the keyboard.

Switches:
/e specifies that an enhanced keyboard is installed
/id: specifies the keyboard in use. |
| label | External - creates or changes the volume identification label on a disc. |
| lastdrive | Internal - CONFIG.SYS - specifies the maximum number of drives you can access. |
| lastdrivehigh | External - causes reserved memory to be removed from the upper memory area (UMA). |
| loadfix | External - forces programs to load above the first 64 KB of conventional memory. |
| loadhigh (lh) | Internal - loads a program into the upper memory area. |
| md (or mkdir) | Internal - creates a new directory on the specified disc. |
| mem | External - it reports the amounts of conventional, expanded and extended memory that are available.

Switches:
/c        displays the status of programs loaded in |

conventional and upper memory area

/d    displays the status of currently loaded programs and of internal drivers

/f    lists the free areas of conventional and upper memory

/m    shows how a program module is currently using memory

/p    pages screen output. Can be used with all the other switches.

**menucolor**    External - CONFIG.SYS - sets the text and background colours for the startup menu.

**menudefault**    External - CONFIG.SYS - specifies the default menu item on the startup menu and sets a time-out value, if needed.

**menuitem**    External - CONFIG.SYS - defines up to nine items on the startup menu.

**mode [options]**    External - sets the mode of operation on a display monitor, parallel/serial printer or the RS232C port. The keyboard repetition and auto-repeat start delay time can be set.

**more**    External - sends output to the console, or window, one screen-full at a time.

Example: type read.me | more

143

|  | displays the contents of the read.me file one screen at a time. |
|---|---|
| move | External - moves one or more files to the specified location. It can also be used to rename files and directories. |
| numlock | Internal - CONFIG.SYS - specifies whether the NUMLOCK key is set ON or OFF. |
| net config | External - displays the controllable network services that are running. |
| net diag | External - displays diagnostic information about your network. |
| net help or net /? | External - provides a list of network commands and topics you can get help with, or provides help with a specific command or topic. |
| net init | External - real mode only - loads protocol and network adapter drivers without binding them. |
| net logoff | External - real mode only - disconnects your computer from the network. Does not work with NetWare NCP servers. |
| net logon | External - real mode only - identifies you as a member of a workgroup. Does not work with NetWare NCP servers. |
| net password | External - real mode only - changes your logon password. Does not work with NetWare NCP servers. |

| | |
|---|---|
| net print | External - displays or controls print jobs. Does not work with NetWare NCP servers. |
| net start | External - real mode only - starts a network service or displays a list of started services. |
| net stop | External - real mode only - stops a network service. |
| net time | External - synchronises the computer's clock with that of a network server or domain. |
| net use | External - connects a computer to or disconnects it from a network shared resource, or displays information about the connections. |
| net ver | External - displays the type and version number of the network redirector being used. |
| net view | External - displays a list of servers on a network or displays the resources being shared by a server. |
| nlsfunc [filename] | External - specifies a file containing country specific information. |
| path | Internal - sets and displays the path to be searched by Windows for external commands or batch files. |
| | Type PATH ; to clear all search-path settings and direct to search only in the current directory. |
| | Type PATH without parameters to display the current path. |

| | |
|---|---|
| pause | Internal - suspends processing of a batch file and displays a message that prompts you to press any key to continue. |
| prompt | Internal - changes the command prompt's appearance. |
| | Example: $p$g |
| | which allows the path of the current working directory to be displayed as the prompt. |
| rd (or rmdir) | Internal - removes the specified directory. |
| rem | Enables you to include comments in batch files. |
| ren (or rename) | Internal - changes the file name. |
| | Example: ren a:\doc\mem1 mem2 |
| | will rename the mem1 file, which is to be found in sub-directory doc on a disc in the a: drive, to mem2. |
| scandisk | External - checks discs and file system for damage and repairs it. Better to carry out this function from Windows system tools. |
| set | Internal - sets strings into the command processor's environment. The general form of the command is: |
| | set [name=[parameter]] |
| | Set by itself displays the current environment. |

| setver | External - displays the version table. |
|---|---|
| shell | Internal - CONFIG.SYS - specifies the name and location of the command interpreter you want Windows 95 to use. |
| shift | Internal - allows more than 10 replaceable parameters in a batch file. |
| smartdrv | External - creates a disc cache in extended memory which speeds up access to your hard disc. **Do NOT place this command in your AUTOEXEC.BAT file, as it will clash with Windows 95.** |

Parameters:

[[drive+|−]  Specifies the letter of the drive for caching control. The plus (+) sign enables caching, while the minus (−) sign disables it. A drive letter without a plus or minus sign, enables read-caching and disables write-caching.

Switches:

/e:size  Specifies in bytes the 'element' size of the cache that moves at a time. Valid values are 1024, 2048, 4096, and 8192 (default is 8192). The larger the size, the more memory is used

/b:size  Specifies the 'buffer' size in kilobytes of the read-ahead buffer - the additional data read by SMARTDrive when an

| | application reads data from the hard disc (default is 16 K) |
|---|---|
| /c | Writes all cached data from memory to disc - use this option if you are going to turn off your computer |
| /r | Clears the contents of the existing cache and restarts SMARTDrive |
| /l | Prevents SMARTDrive from automatically loading into upper memory blocks, even if these are available. You can use the /l switch if upper memory is enabled for use by programs |
| /q | Suppresses status messages when SMARTDrive starts. The /q switch cannot be used with the /v switch |
| /v | Display status and error messages when starting. (By default, SMARTDrive does not display any messages unless it encounters an error condition.) The /v switch cannot be used with the /q switch |
| /s | Displays extra information about SMARTDrive's status. |
| sort [filespec] | External - reads data from the screen or a file, sorts it and sends it to the screen, a file or other device. |

Switches:
/r     sorts in reverse order
/+n   sorts the file according to the
        character in column n
command - specifies a command
        whose output is to be sorted.

Example: dir | sort

sorts the output of the *dir* command in alphabetical order.

stacks(high)  Internal - CONFIG.SYS - supports
the dynamic use of data stacks to
handle hardware interrupts.

start  External - runs a Windows program or a DOS program.

Switches:
/m      Run the new program
        minimised    (in    the
        background)
/max   Run the new program
        maximised    (in    the
        foreground)
/r       Run the new program in
        the foreground, the default
/w      Does not return until the
        other program exits.

submenu  Internal - CONFIG.SYS - defines
an item on a startup menu that,
when selected, displays another
set of options.

subst  External - allows substitution of a
virtual drive for an existing drive
and path.

Switch:
/d  deletes a virtual drive.

Example: subst d: a:\wproc\docs

will cause future reference to drive d: to be taken as replacement to the longer reference to a:\wproc\docs.

| | |
|---|---|
| switches | Internal - specifies Windows options from within your CONFIG.SYS file . |
| sys | External - transfers the Windows 95 system files from the logged drive to the disc in the specified drive. |
| time | Internal - displays and sets the system time. It also supports a 12- or 24-hour format. |
| type | Internal - displays the contents of a file on the screen. |
| ver | Internal - displays the operating system version number. |
| verify | Internal - allows the verify switch to be turned ON or OFF. |
| | Example: verify OFF |
| vol | Internal - displays the disc volume label, if it exists. |
| xcopy [filespec] | External - copies files and direct-ories, including lower level sub-directories if they exist, to the des-tination drive and directory. |

Switches:

/a copies source files that have their archive bit set

/c ignores errors

/d copies source files which were modified on or after a specified date

/e copies sub-directories even if they are empty - use this switch in conjunction with /s and /t

/f displays all filenames during the copy process

/h copies hidden and system files

/i forces creation of new directory, if named destination does not exist

/k retains read only attribute in copied files. By default this does not happen

/l displays a list of files that will be copied

/m copies archived files only, but also turns off the archive bit in the source file

/n copies using aliases, or short file names

/p prompts the user with '(Y/N)?'

/q suppresses message display

/r copies over read only files

/s copies directories and their sub-directories unless they are empty

/t copies only the tree, not the contained files

/v causes verification of each file as it is written. Not actually needed with Windows 95

/w displays a message before starting to copy.

# APPENDIX A
# KEYBOARD SHORTCUTS

The following actions are the standard shortcuts for working with objects in the Windows 95 interface. Most use the keyboard only, but some involve the mouse as well.

## General Keyboard-Only Commands

| Shortcut | Action |
|---|---|
| F1 | Start Help |
| F10 | Go to menu mode |
| Shift+F10 | Display context menu for selected item |
| Ctrl+Esc | Display START menu and move the focus to the taskbar |
| Ctrl+Esc, Esc | Move the focus on the taskbar so you can use TAB and then Shift+F10 for context menu, or use TAB and arrow key to change tasks, or use TAB to go to the desktop |
| Alt+Tab | Switch to the next running application |
| Alt+M | When the focus is on the taskbar or desktop, minimize all windows and move the focus to the desktop |
| Alt+S | When no windows are open and no items are selected on the desktop, display the Start menu; then use arrow keys to select menu commands. |

## Shortcuts for a Selected Object

| Shortcut | Action |
|---|---|
| F2 | Rename |
| F3 | Find |
| Ctrl+X | Cut |
| Ctrl+C | Copy |
| Ctrl+V | Paste |

| | |
|---|---|
| Delete | Delete |
| Shift+Delete | Delete file immediately without putting it in Recycle Bin |
| Alt+Enter | Display properties |
| Alt+dble-click | Display properties |
| Ctrl+right-click | Place alternative commands on the context menu (Open With) |
| Shift+dble-click | Explore an object; if the object does not have an Explore command, this starts the default action (usually the Open command). |

## Shortcuts with Folders and Windows Explorer

| *Shortcut* | *Action* |
|---|---|
| F5 | Refresh display |
| Ctrl+Z | Undo |
| Ctrl+A | Select All |
| Backspace | Go to the parent folder |

*In Explorer only*

| | |
|---|---|
| F4 | Display the combo box and move the input focus to the list |
| F6 | Move the focus between panes |
| Ctrl+G | Choose the Go To command |

*In the Explorer Tree*

| | |
|---|---|
| * (num keypad) | Expand everything under the selection |
| + (num keypad) | Expand the selection |
| − (num keypad) | Collapse the selection |
| → | Expand the current selection if it is not expanded; otherwise, go to the first child |
| ← | Collapse current selection if it is expanded; otherwise, go to the parent |
| Ctrl+arrow key | Scroll without moving the selection. |

# Shortcuts in Open and Save Dialogue Boxes

| Shortcut | Action |
|----------|--------|
| F4 | Display the Look In list |
| F5 | Refresh the view |
| Backspace | Go to the parent folder if the focus is on the View window |

# General Shortcuts

| To | Action Required |
|----|-----------------|
| Copy a file | Press the Ctrl key while you drag the file to a folder. |
| Create a shortcut | Press the <Ctrl+Shift> keys while you drag the file to the desktop or to a folder. |
| Close current and all parent folders | Press Shift key and click the Close button on the folder. |
| Tab through the pages in a properties box | Press the <Ctrl+Shift+TAB> keys or, more simply, <Ctrl+TAB>. |
| Bypass Auto-Run when inserting a compact disc | Press the Shift key when inserting the disc. |

# APPENDIX B
# SUPPORTED QUICK VIEWERS

At the time of writing, Quick Viewers for the following file formats were currently available, and shipped on the Windows 95 CD-ROM (disc users can download the Quick Viewers from on-line sources, or can apply direct to Microsoft).

Most independent software developers should be producing viewers for their programs to make them more usable with Windows 95.

| Format | Type of file |
|--------|--------------|
| .ASC | ASCII files |
| .BMP | Windows Bitmap Graphics |
| .CDR | Corel Draw |
| .DIB | Windows Bitmap Graphics |
| .DLL | Dynamic Link Libraries |
| .DOC | Word for MS-DOS versions 5 and 6 |
| | Word for Windows versions 2 and 6 |
| | WordPerfect versions 4.2, 5, 6, and 6.1 |
| .DRW | Micrographix Draw |
| .EXE | Executable files |
| .INF | Setup files |
| .INI | Configuration files |
| .MOD | Multiplan versions 3, 4.0, and 4.1 |
| .PPT | PowerPoint version 4 |
| .PRE | Freelance for Windows |
| .RLE | Bitmap files (RunLengthEncoding) |
| .RTF | Rich Text Format |
| .SAM | Ami and Ami Pro |
| .TXT | Text files |
| .WB1 | Quattro Pro for Windows spreadsheet |
| .WDB | Works database |
| .WK1 | Lotus 1-2-3 Release 1 and 2 |
| .WK3 | Lotus 1-2-3 Release 3 |
| .WK4 | Lotus 1-2-3 Release 4 spreadsheet and chart |
| .WKS | Lotus 1-2-3 Release 1A |
| | Microsoft Works version 3 |
| .WMF | Windows Metafiles |

| | |
|---|---|
| .WPD | WordPerfect demo files |
| .WPS | Works word processing |
| .WQ1 | Quattro Pro for MS-DOS |
| .WQ2 | Quattro Pro version 5 for MS-DOS |
| .WRI | Windows 3.x Write |
| .XLC | Excel 4 chart |
| .XLS | Excel 4 spreadsheet |
| | Excel 5 spreadsheet and chart |

# APPENDIX C
# SYSTEM FILES AND SETTINGS

The following is a brief overview of the system files used by Windows 95 when it starts operation, and how they compare with those used by your previous DOS version. Most readers could quite happily ignore the next few pages, but if you are struggling to get a 'difficult' MS-DOS game to use the full facilities of your system, you might find them useful.

## Original System Files

The following table shows how Setup renames the old system files for the previous operating system when Windows 95 is first installed. They are thus available for possible future use, if you revert back to your previous set-up.

| Original MS-DOS filename | Renamed filename |
|---|---|
| autoexec.bat | autoexec.dos |
| command.com | command.dos |
| config.sys | config.dos |
| io.sys (or ibmbio.com) | io.dos |
| mode.com | mode_dos.com |
| msdos.sys (or ibmdos.com) | msdos.dos |

## New System Files

The following 'new' files are used by Windows 95.

## IO.SYS:

Windows 95 uses a new system file, IO.SYS, which replaces the two MS-DOS system files (IO.SYS and MSDOS.SYS). This real-mode operating system file contains the information needed to start your computer. The files, CONFIG.SYS and AUTOEXEC.BAT are no longer needed to start the Windows 95 operating system (but they are kept for backward compatibility with certain applications and drivers).

The following drivers are loaded by default in IO.SYS, if these files are found on the hard disc:

```
HIMEM.SYS
IFSHLP.SYS
SETVER.EXE
DBLSPACE.BIN or DRVSPACE.BIN
```

Most of the functions provided by the various CONFIG.SYS file entries are now provided by default in IO.SYS, as listed below:

| Setting | Description |
| --- | --- |
| dos=high | Specifies that MS-DOS should be loaded in the high memory area (HMA). Also, the umb value is included if EMM386 is loaded from CONFIG.SYS. (IO.SYS does not load EMM386.) |
| himem.sys | Enables access to the HMA. This line loads and runs the real-mode Memory Manager. HIMEM.SYS is loaded by default in Windows 95. |
| ifshlp.sys | Installable File System Helper, which loads device drivers. This allows the system to make file system calls. Until this is loaded, only the minimal file system from IO.SYS is used. After this point, the full file system is available. |
| setver.exe | Optional TSR-type device, included for compatibility reasons. Some MS-DOS based applications require a specific version of MS-DOS to be running. This file responds to applications that query for the version number and sets the version number required. |
| files= | Specifies the number of file handle buffers to create. This is specifically for files opened using MS-DOS calls and is not required by Windows 95. It |

is included for compatibility with older applications. The default value is 60.

lastdrive=
Specifies the last drive letter available for assignment. This is not required for Windows 95 but is included for compatibility with older applications. If Windows 95 Setup finds this entry, it is moved to the Registry. The default value is z.

buffers=
Specifies the number of file buffers to create. This is specifically for applications using IO.SYS calls and is not required by Windows 95. The default value is 30.

stacks=
Specifies the number and size of stack frames. This is not required for Windows 95 but is included for compatibility with older applications. The default value is 9,256.

shell=command.com
Indicates what command process to use. By default, the /p switch is included to indicate that the command process is permanent and should not be unloaded. If the /p switch is not specified, AUTOEXEC.BAT is not processed and the command process can be unloaded when quitting the operating system.

fcbs=
Specifies the number of file control blocks that can be open at the same time. You should use a fcbs= line in CONFIG.SYS only if you have an older program that requires such a setting. The default value is 4.

The values in IO.SYS cannot be edited, to override its default values, you should place an entry in the CONFIG.SYS file with the value you want.

## MSDOS.SYS:
Windows 95 Setup creates a hidden, read-only system file named MSDOS.SYS in the root of the computer's boot drive. This file contains important paths used to locate other Windows files, including the Registry, and is also created for compatibility with applications that require it to be present before they can be installed.

MSDOS.SYS also supports an [Options] section, which you can add to and edit to customise the start-up process.

## CONFIG.SYS:
Windows 95 has changed the method of handling the two files CONFIG.SYS and AUTOEXEC.BAT during system startup. Most of their previous functions are now automatically carried out using IO.SYS and the Registry.

CONFIG.SYS can contain application-specific entries in addition to information stored in IO.SYS. These are processed in the order listed, after the base CONFIG.SYS file has been read, all devices are loaded, and COMMAND.COM is running.

If you edit CONFIG.SYS in Windows 95 remember the following:

Do not include the **smartdrv** command. Disc-caching is now built-in.

Windows 95 also includes built-in mouse support, so remove any **device=mouse.sys,** or similar, lines.

## AUTOEXEC.BAT:
AUTOEXEC.BAT is included for compatibility purposes. If your computer has an AUTOEXEC.BAT file, each line is processed in sequence during system start up. AUTOEXEC.BAT can contain additional application-specific entries that are run in the sequence they are listed.

The default Windows 95 environment includes the following,
AUTOEXEC.BAT commands:

```
tmp=c:\windows\temp
temp=c:\windows\temp
prompt=$p$g
path=c:\windows;c:\windows\command
comspec=c:\windows\command\command.com
```

If you edit AUTOEXEC.BAT, you should follow these basic
guidelines:

- Do not include other versions of Windows in the path.

- Start the path statement with
  C:\WINDOWS;C:\WINDOWS\COMMAND

- Windows 95 Setup leaves your previous MS-DOS
  directory in the path. Do not change this.

- Do not add SMARTDrive, or other disc caches.

- Do not include any statements for loading mouse
  software.

## SYSTEM.INI and WIN.INI:
Most configuration options for Windows 95 are now stored in
the Registry and are no longer required in the SYSTEM.INI
and WIN.INI files.

## BOOTLOG.TXT:
The BOOTLOG.TXT file is created during Setup when the
Windows 95 operating system is first started, and contains a
record of the current start up process for the system. It
shows the Windows 95 components and drivers loaded and
initialised, and the status of each.
  If you use the F8 option for interactive system start up, you
can choose to create a boot log during system start up.

## The Registry

Windows 95 uses a central location, called the Registry, to store information previously held in the .INI files used by earlier versions of Windows.

The Registry is structured as a hierarchical database to store text or binary value information and maintains all of the configuration parameters previously stored in the three Windows system files, WIN.INI, SYSTEM.INI, and PROTOCOL.INI, and other application-specific .INI files.

Like the CONFIG.SYS and AUTOEXEC.BAT files, these INI files are still used for compatibility reasons. Hopefully developers of new Windows 95 applications will, in the future, use the Registry to consolidate their application-specific information.

To take a look in your Registry, type the command REGEDIT into the START, **Run** text box.

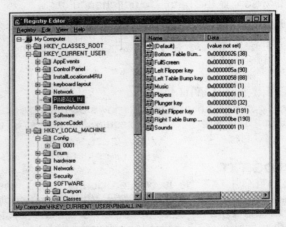

When new Plug and Play devices are installed, the system checks the existing configuration in the Registry to determine which hardware resources are not being used, so that the new device can be properly configured without conflicting with a device already installed in the system.

We would not recommend you making any changes in your Registry, unless you are very happy about what you are doing.

# INDEX

# NOTES

**NOTES**

# NOTES

# NOTES

# COMPANION DISC TO THIS BOOK

This book contains several example file listings. There is no reason why you should type them yourself into your computer, unless you wish to do so, or need the practice.

The COMPANION DISC comes with these listings, as well as a GLOSSARY that would not fit in the book.

COMPANION DISCS for most books written by the same author(s) and published by BERNARD BABANI (publishing) LTD, are also available and are listed at the front of this book. **Make sure you fill in your name and address** and specify the book number and title in your order.

## ORDERING INSTRUCTIONS

To obtain your copy of the companion disc, fill in the order form below, or a copy of it, enclose a cheque (payable to **P.R.M. Oliver**) or a postal order, and send it to the address given below.

| Book No. | Book Name | Unit Price | Total Price |
|---|---|---|---|
| BP 400 | Windows 95 Explained | £3.50 | |
| BP ........ | | £3.50 | |
| BP ........ | | £3.50 | |
| Name ................................ | | Sub-total | £............. |
| Address ................................. | | P & P (@ 45p/disc) | £............. |
| | | Total Due | £............. |
| Send to: P.R.M. Oliver, CSM, Pool, Redruth, Cornwall, TR15 3SE | | | |

**PLEASE NOTE**

The author(s) are fully responsible for providing this Companion Disc service. The publishers of this book accept no responsibility for the supply, quality, or magnetic contents of the disc, or in respect of any damage, or injury that might be suffered or caused by its use.